REIMAGINE CHANGE

Grammar Factory Publishing
MacMillan Company Limited
25 Telegram Mews, 39th Floor, Suite 3906
Toronto, Ontario, Canada
M5V 3Z1

www.grammarfactory.com

Lancaster, Ciara
    Reimagine Change: Escape change fatigue, build resilience and awaken your creative brilliance / Ciara Lancaster

Includes index.
ISBN 978-1-989737-09-5

    1. BUS085000 BUSINESS & ECONOMICS / Organizational Behavior.
    2. BUS107000 BUSINESS & ECONOMICS / Personal Success.
    3. SEL024000 SELF-HELP / Self-Management / Stress Management.

A catalogue record for this book is available from the National Library of Australia.

NATIONAL
LIBRARY
OF AUSTRALIA

Production Credits
Printed in 2020 by McPherson's Printing Group
Cover design by Designerbility
Interior layout design by Dania Zafar
Book production and editorial services by Grammar Factory Publishing

Disclaimer

REIMAGINE CHANGE

ESCAPE CHANGE FATIGUE,

BUILD RESILIENCE

AND AWAKEN YOUR CREATIVE BRILLIANCE

CIARA LANCASTER

CONTENTS

Dedication   vii

Acknowledgements   viii

INTRODUCTION: Overloaded, overwhelmed and over it   1

A Word on Part 1   19

PART 1: KNOW   **23**

CHAPTER 1: REALISE your reality   25

CHAPTER 2: RESPOND via your capability   49

CHAPTER 3: RECLAIM your brain   73

From Part 1 to Part 2   99

PART 2: GROW   **103**

CHAPTER 4: REGENERATE your body   105

CHAPTER 5: RECODE your mind   143

CHAPTER 6: REIMAGINE your creativity   177

Conclusion   219

Beyond The Pages   225

Sources   227

About The Author   235

DEDICATION

This poem is dedicated to honouring the past, persevering in the present and welcoming transition in the future.

'THE GUEST HOUSE' BY JELALUDDIN RUMI

This being human is a guest house.
Every morning a new arrival.
A joy, a depression, a meanness,
some momentary awareness comes
as an unexpected visitor.
Welcome and entertain them all!
Even if they are a crowd of sorrows,
who violently sweep your house
empty of its furniture,
still, treat each guest honourably.
He may be clearing you out
for some new delight.
The dark thought, the shame, the malice,
Meet them at the door laughing
and invite them in.
Be grateful for whatever comes,
Because each has been sent
as a guide from beyond.

ACKNOWLEDGEMENTS

Writing a book is a very solitary experience. Within those hours of deep work, you are trusting your mind to reach in so many new directions – from researching to writing content to designing models.

Then there is the dance between what you want to articulate versus attending to the questions your reader may be asking during each chapter. One might consider it the ultimate mental tennis match. Between so-called 'sets', everything feels more effortless when you have an inner circle keeping your spirits high and tank refuelled.

Thank you to my author coach, Kelly Irving. You played such a pivotal role in getting those visual ideas out of my head and into a structured book plan. Your deep understanding of the emotional trials and tribulations that an author endures made all the difference.

Thank you to my editorial and publishing team, Michelle Stevenson, Jake Creasey, Julia Kuris and Scott MacMillan. You made the complex simple and kept me laser-focused on connecting with the reader and getting the book launched.

Additional shout-outs to Ellie Schroeder for the wonderful illustrations within the book, to Nikki Malvar for my author photograph and to Tina Tower for my website. You are all so talented in your areas of expertise!

Thank you to Dr. Stephen Porges. Steve, it is an honour to have connected. Your ground-breaking research is so incredibly impactful in understanding human connection.

Thank you to past colleagues and clients for sharing your 'What's keeping you up at night?' stories off the record. Those conversations fuelled my desire to find a way to share learnings with others experiencing similar dis-ease in the workplace.

Thank you to the thought leaders and fellow authors for paving the way and spurring me on to share this work with a broader audience.

Thank you to my dear friends, the ones that encouraged me out for a late-night drink, an early-morning walk or a night away when regeneration was required. Having shoulders to lean on through the good times and the challenging times is everything.

Most of all, thank you to my immediate family and parents, Roger and Oonagh.

To Luke, for holding down the fort and for giving me the space to regenerate and create. Bring on the next book...I mean the next chapter of our lives together.

Thanks to my children, Toby and Andrew. I am so proud to be your mum and I look forward to seeing your unique ways of tackling all the change that lies ahead for you. I will fondly remember all of the moments that kept me going in between writing sets, including shooting hoops, kitchen dance-offs, games of Uno and reading *Harry Potter* together.

Finally, thank you to you, dear reader, for trusting me to guide you through to better outcomes than where you are at right now. Let's do this!

INTRODUCTION

OVERLOADED, OVERWHELMED AND OVER IT

'It's not the mountain we conquer, but ourselves.'

– SIR EDMUND HILLARY, ONE OF THE FIRST CLIMBERS
TO REACH THE SUMMIT OF MOUNT EVEREST IN 1953

As a Change Manager at Deloitte Touche Tohmatsu in Sydney, Australia, one component of the role involved conducting change leadership interviews with both leaders and employees to gather data on the current state of play. In other words, listening to what is and isn't said about past, present and future change and business transformation initiatives. Collecting and assessing qualitative and quantitative data is a crucial component of organisational diagnostics.

With that in mind, let me tell you a story about a man named Jack. (Please note that some of the examples or case studies in this book have been anonymised, adapted or fictionalised for privacy, at the request of the subject, or for illustrative purposes.) One day, I had just sat down to conduct a change leadership interview with

Jack when the tirade began. Jack appeared angry and wanted to get straight to the crux of the matter at hand, which, in this case, was in relation to a business transformation project.

'What you need to convey to the leadership team and those consultants is that the last business transformation project didn't exactly go as smoothly as we had been promised. For those of us on the receiving end of it, it felt like the Kokoda Track of the corporate world,' he said.

(A note to international readers: For Australians, the Kokoda Track holds a special significance – this is where Australian servicemen and women fought the Japanese during World War Two. For seven months, soldiers fought in treacherous jungle conditions. What they endured was absolutely brutal; our soldiers simply could not have been prepared for the physical and emotional challenge.)

After the meeting, Jack went into overdrive. He issued details about kick-off meetings, with flashy presentations outlining the new business priorities, how the entire business was expected to 'get on board' and 'buy in' to the latest set of directives, how his team was delegated extra work and additional training on top of an already heavy workload, how office 'quick wins' were not communicating the reality of what was *really* taking place on the floor, and so on.

Tensions continued to build over the next few months, and people began to wonder whether the streamlining and new technology would result in the loss of their jobs and their livelihoods. Jack's once vibrant team began to experience transformation PTSD (post-traumatic stress disorder) in the forms of chronic stress, change fatigue and burnout. Adding salt to their wounds, exiting team members were not replaced, yet company press releases and management meetings continued to focus on the organisation's record revenue year.

Mark Zuckerberg's famous mantra of 'move fast and break things' had done just that. The humans were broken, mentally fragile and disconnected. Work that once lit them up now had the opposite effect. From a business perspective, data confirmed that employee engagement had dipped to an all-time low, and this was starting to impact retention, productivity and innovation efforts.

Underneath his corporate bravado, Jack himself was feeling the three Os: overloaded, overwhelmed and over it. He wanted to provide more support to his team but felt that he was not equipped with the right change terminology, nor did he have the capacity or energy to commit to each team member while working on his own client work. Something needed to be done to better support the change and psychological suffering taking place.

Jack didn't seek out support for himself, either. The risks associated with that were too high. His boss might view him as a weak leader, his competitive co-workers couldn't be trusted as they were gunning for his job, and it was common knowledge that the human resources team was compliance-focused and typically acted on behalf of the organisation's best interest, rather than that of each individual employee.

Things were pretty frosty on the home front, too. Jack's wife was less than impressed with his non-existent work-life balance. The children desperately craved his presence and participation. Work functions and work calls took place at all hours of the night, and the weekend was consumed by Jack catching up on work.

Jack found it hard to switch off and get a decent night's sleep. He was troubled by late-night rumination of work scenarios playing on repeat in his mind. Poor Jack kept the negative cycle looping by using the justification that he was just 'under the pump' like everyone else. It seemed like there was no end in sight – but Jack felt he had no choice but to keep pushing on.

Does this scenario sound familiar? Perhaps you have experienced or are experiencing something similar? You're not alone.

Research and data confirm that what many executive-level professionals are experiencing is part of a wider change overload and burnout epidemic. According to a *Harvard Business Review* article, which referenced a Harvard Medical School research study, '*nine-ty-six percent of all senior leaders have experienced some degree of burnout, and one third described their condition as extreme (severe burnout).*'

Another *Forbes* article explored the ways in which leadership burnout begets employee burnout, stating that '*workplace wellness programs have failed to improve people's health much at all.*' The article also states:

> '*What leaders say and do has a disproportionate impact on the behaviours that employees feel comfortable adopting. Even with the proliferation of nap rooms, yoga classes, and mindfulness courses, if leaders don't sanction and model the use of these offerings, employees are loath to utilise them.*'

Regardless of your title or your tenure, it appears that no one is immune to the devastating physical and psychological impacts brought on by change overload and burnout.

But the dogma of 'shareholder profits above all else' is now antiquated. According to the 2020 Edelman Trust Barometer report, *'eighty-seven percent of respondents said that customers, employees and communities are more important than shareholders to a company's long-term success.'*

This indicates that the paradigm shift is coming and this demands a duty of care imperative. Are you waiting for your organisation and leadership team to address your burnout? They're not. At least, not soon enough. Fair or not, the onus is on you to take ownership and make damn sure that you are resilient, ready and resourceful to lead yourself through change.

IT'S TIME TO **REIMAGINE CHANGE**

This book is intended to expose the human impact associated with continuous change in the workplace, and provide compassion and emotional optimism to liberate you – as an aspiring change leader – to shift in a more positive direction.

With change comes opportunity. The more open, adaptive and resilient you are to change, the more opportunities you will have access to. However, when the fear alarm is sounding, it makes it rather challenging to focus on future possibilities.

Ask yourself: Do you have what it takes to optimally cope and thrive in the future workplace, or are all the signs pointing towards you being ill-equipped?

- How will you respond to exponential change in your personal and professional life?
- What strategies will you adopt to better support yourself as well as those people around you?
- Is your current contribution at work congruent with your potential?

The ultimate aim of *Reimagine Change* is to support you to change how you regenerate and then reapproach the incremental waves of change coming your way. And if you are not feeling any incremental workplace pressure, then that in itself presents a new set of issues that we will explore in future chapters.

By the end of *Reimagine Change*, you will have discovered:

- That complaining about your work circumstances does you zero favours
- How to remove assumptions, fears and insecurities that are holding you back
- How to anticipate, evolve and better contribute to change
- The key change identities that will influence your success
- The intrapersonal skills required for energy and intentional change
- How to balance your executive and emotional brain
- How to reframe and better respond to change
- How to forget about endgames and focus on process and progress

Unfortunately, the corporate world can be very polarising. Either you end up with an overinflated ego and a deep sense of disconnection, or you limit your potential by not playing the game and fitting a preconceived mould of who you need to be to get ahead.

Do not allow past negative experiences of workplace change to deter you on your path to potential. Do not let assumptions, fears or insecurities hold you back. And do not suffer in silence; there are outlets of support, one of which is this book.

I have written this book as a support system, or toolkit, for you to draw upon and mould to suit your own needs and desires. My hope is that you will use these insights to launch yourself towards progress and potential fulfilment.

So, on that note, allow me to introduce myself properly – and explain why I wrote this book, the content it contains and why I think it's so valuable.

TAKE IT FROM SOMEONE WHO'S BEEN THERE

My name is Ciara Lancaster.

I believe that the world can be an incredibly different place when you return home from work with a positively charged mind and heart. The key to achieving this in the current, complex environment is change capability.

Change capability is about enhancing your humanness and your contribution to better yourself and the organisations that you devote so much time to. In order to successfully evolve and thrive in the workplace, you need to upgrade your individual change capability at a speed equal to or greater than the expected pace of technology upskilling. Genuinely *being with* and *being for* people is at the core of human belonging and connection. You need to understand what this means within yourself before you can expand the energy outward to others.

Leaders at all levels are now expected to assume the role of change advocate. Even if you don't necessarily have the word 'change' in your job title, do you find that issues like change fatigue, resistance and mental health pressures are negatively impacting employee engagement, culture and retention? If the answer is yes, then *Reimagine Change* will act as your go-to guide to transition you from sub-optimal, corporate co-dependency to a self-directed coaching model grounded in the regeneration, recoding and reimagining of your psychological capital.

Fred Luthans, organisational behaviour expert and author of *Psychological Capital*, explores psychological capital as a state that unlocks performance, uncovers potential and encourages positive leadership interactivity. Luthans' research found that a person's performance is determined not only by intellectual capital and social capital but also their psychological capital, which is based on the four 'open to development' elements of hope, self-efficacy, resilience and optimism.

Having held senior leadership roles in organisational change management, sales and strategy, I've witnessed firsthand the need for such a transition – and the enormous difference it can make not only on an individual level but on an organisational level, too. In addition to Deloitte, I've worked for News Corp, Bauer Media and Southern Cross Austereo.

After spending nearly twenty years in the corporate world, I created *Reimagine Change* to bridge the gap between organisational and personal transformation, focusing specifically on transition from change overload and burnout to designing a new way to *Reimagine Change*.

In among all that, I've also experienced burnout myself. There was a two-year period of my life where I experienced what I call 'peak stretch'. Peak stretch activities for me included:

- Leaping into a new industry
- Starting a new career
- Designing company-first initiatives
- Gaining new academic qualifications
- Broadening my family commitments
- Moving house twice during this time

Yes, all this, while being a mum to two boys under the age of five. This is very common in Sydney and other cities around the world, so by no means am I any different to the majority of hardworking women out there right now. And to combat all this newness, my demise was relying on old coping strategies and being oblivious to the level of control my subconscious mind – the part of the mind that influences unconscious decision making – has on behaviours and outcomes. Since then, I have replaced peak stretch with optimal growth, and the difference has been incredible. But let's keep it real. I'll be the first to admit that I am not infallible. I still have not so great days like everyone else. However, the process with which I move through them is far more fluid.

I'm a big believer that some people talk, some people walk and some people create value offerings for other human beings. Our common humanity and duty of care to one another are the foundations of this work. If you're looking to *Reimagine Change* in business and beyond, I believe I can help you. In addition to working in the corporate world and experiencing burnout myself, here are four more reasons why our paths may align:

1. I VALUE 'JUST LIKE ME' ROLE MODELS

As you now know, I've been on the same corporate Kokoda Track you are probably suffering along right now. And each time, I have either succeeded and levelled up or I have failed and learned. Something I believe you can achieve, too.

2. I VALUE FAMILY

I'm committed to playing an active, nurturing role for my partner and two sons. Parenting is by far the greatest coaching-in-action experience. Nothing lights me up more than seeing my children be curious and creative.

3. I VALUE MASTERY

I've worked alongside the best of the best, most recently as a former Change Manager with Deloitte, all the while continuously upskilling at Sydney University, the University of New South Wales, the Stanford Centre for Compassion and Altruism Research and Education, and The Mind Academy.

4. I VALUE HUMAN POTENTIAL

Like so many others, I have been exposed to toxic bosses that encourage you to shrink and play it small. It is disempowering and unjustified. I want to empower you to flip the script, exploring the possibilities and potential not only for yourself but for others, too.

INTRODUCING THE
REIMAGINE CHANGE MODEL

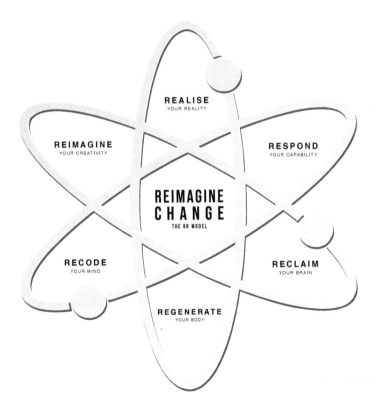

Figure 1: The 6R model to Reimagine Change.

In *Reimagine Change*, you'll discover a framework for addressing, understanding and overcoming change overload and burnout. This model provides insights and methods to help you support yourself via intrapersonal upskilling. This is the information that they don't teach at business school, that is not detailed in traditional leadership curriculums. This is where you benefit from being guided by someone with hands-on life and corporate experience in this area.

The 6R model to *Reimagine Change* consists of the following:

1. REALISE your reality
2. RESPOND via your capability
3. RECLAIM your brain
4. REGENERATE your body
5. RECODE your mind
6. REIMAGINE your creativity

The model may look nice and neat, but don't be fooled by the promise of quick fixes. You will need to invest the necessary time, effort and focus to yield any type of results. While each dimension can be tackled separately, I recommend that the sequencing is adhered to, to de-risk the 'snapback effect' or a return to change overload and burnout. By conquering the six dimensions in the order they appear, you will increase your prosilience (how you intentionally prepare to deal with challenges); resilience (how you bounce back from adversity); and adaptiveness (how you pivot for greater effectiveness) for future change success.

We'll look at each dimension in much more detail in the chapters that follow. The book is divided into two parts, with the first three Rs in Part 1 and the remaining three in Part 2. For now, here's a brief outline, so you know what to expect at each stage:

REALISE signals the rapid descent into the depths of change overload and burnout. This is the realisation of what is taking place, why it is taking place, and the negative impact for organisations and, more importantly, human beings. The key question to consider is: What is this teaching me?

RESPOND signals the shift to being curious about showing up differently and planning to take action. This is about responding to the opportunity at hand by acknowledging sub-optimal functioning and being accountable for rebuilding a future-focused change identity. The key question to consider is: What would future me ask current me to start now?

RECLAIM signals the shift from hyper-alert, survival brain to a calmer, self-regulated brain. This is about befriending your brain and recognising that knowledge about brain behaviour provides a powerful foundation. The key question to consider is: What brain enrichment strategy do I need to adopt?

REGENERATE signals the need for respite. To regenerate means to acknowledge that the human body and mind are not machines and that, for people over profits to become a reality, an initial period of in-depth recovery is essential. The key question to consider is: What environmental, human or psychological influences are no longer serving me?

RECODE signals the desire to accelerate your change capability. You've come this far, but are you willing to go the extra mile? Recoding requires you to break through to the subconscious mind and install new, change-capable mindsets for success. The key question to consider is: What belief systems are limiting my personal change acceleration?

REIMAGINE signals the return of emotional presence and energy. You will need to decide how best to channel this into creative endeavours that count. The key question to consider is: What creative value will I draw on to contribute to my work, my community and my life?

The sequencing of the six-part framework is designed to reflect how individuals spiral 'up and out' with regard to change overload and burnout. In a world of busyness, brain fog and cognitive overload, you may be inclined to default to shortcuts, tips and tricks, and quick wins. However, these rarely support long-term human sustainability and potential fulfilment. Instead, they keep you hooked on bad habits, negative beliefs and co-dependent programming that no longer serves you. It's time to evolve.

Reimagine Change is based upon a multi-disciplinary approach, underpinned by academic research, thought leadership, and first-hand change leadership and personal transformation experiences. Figure 2 (opposite) provides an overview of what this entails.

As you can see, the multi-disciplinary approach to *Reimagine Change* consists of:
1. Change psychology
2. Neuroscientific insights
3. Neuro-linguistic programming
4. Burnout regeneration
5. Compassion cultivation
6. Change management

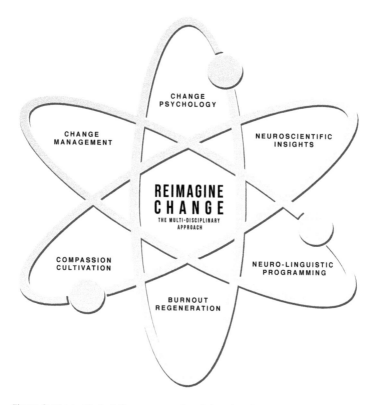

Figure 2: The multi-disciplinary approach to Reimagine Change.

My goal is to provide you with the necessary support if you find yourself under siege from change overload and burnout. This book has been designed to provide you with actionable mindset insights, emotional resilience and the change capability to thrive in the future.

I BELIEVE IN YOU

Throughout the book, I will share personal stories that have shaped who I am today. Through this role-modelling practice, my hope is that you, too, will be courageous enough to share more of your stories with team members and loved ones as a way to connect and build collective resilience.

Humans are hardwired to share stories. Stories provide authentic examples of who and what we are, not just what we say. They can also provide valuable lessons and serve as inspiration. I grew up across the road from the Sydney Cricket Ground. Dad used to take my two siblings and me to *all* the cricket matches. Test matches could be particularly slow for young enthusiasts. So, in between eating ice creams, collecting bat signatures and laughing along to Merv Hughes' stretching antics, dad would explain the intricacies of the game and tell us lots of stories about the players.

As the years went on, my favourite story became the one about the boy who loved playing cricket from a very young age. Both of his parents were busy with work commitments, so the boy's grandmother took it upon herself to pay for and take the young boy to the weekly cricket training. The story goes that the grand-mother sewed a special label inside of the boy's cricket top. The label read 'A future Australian cricket captain' and was a constant reminder of his potential.

The course of that boy's life changed forever when someone believed in him enough to nurture both his mindset and talents, and he did indeed pursue a career in professional cricket. That boy went on to be the only Australian cricket captain to lead his team to three successful Ashes victories during the golden era of cricket between 2004 and 2011. That boy is Ricky Ponting. If you're a cricket fan, you may remember that when Ponting's grandmother died in 2011, the Australian cricket team wore black armbands to honour her.

Why am I telling you this? Because in life and work, sometimes all it takes to start on the road to success is another person to believe in you before you can believe in yourself. This is particularly common as a way of encouraging young children. However, what happens when you grow up? Unfortunately, in today's society, we are seeing a rise in isolation, busyness, flexible working and living alone, making genuine, ongoing connection a challenge for many of us. If that's your reality, then remember that I believe in you and that this book is designed to nudge you in a positive direction.

So, whatever happened to Merv Hughes? Well, he is long retired but has been known to hand out the occasional baggy, green cap to players on debut and is quoted as saying, *'There is an emu and kangaroo on the front of your hat. They never take a step backwards, and I know you won't, either.'* With that in mind, let's find out if you are ready to take your first step forward to *Reimagine Change.*

A WORD ON PART I

'The real voyage of discovery consists not in seeking
new landscapes, but in having new eyes.'
– MARCEL PROUST

L et's be honest – 'change' is often a despised word. This is largely because so many people have witnessed – and suffered from – poorly managed change. While change management practices have begun to be more human-centric out of necessity, it is often the leadership team and broader cadence of the business that lags lightyears behind. In a world of busyness, change is viewed as burdensome.

As I explained in the introduction, this book is divided into two parts: Part 1 and Part 2. Part 1 is titled 'KNOW', as it's designed to help you grasp the gravity of the situation you are in, both in the workplace and in your head. This will help orient you, so that you can forge a new path for yourself and ultimately achieve success. The focus here is to use data-driven findings and academic insights to enhance your thinking and reflecting time. It is only when the 'what' and the 'why' are compelling enough that you will become ready to take action.

Here are some questions to keep in mind as you move through each chapter in Part 1:

REALISE your reality: What is the depth of your emotional experience of change? Chapter 1 gives you permission to re-experience the dark side of change.

RESPOND via your capability: What might your best next step forward be? Don't leave choices to chance. Chapter 2 asks you to draw a line in the sand.

RECLAIM your brain: How might befriending your brain benefit your journey? Chapter 3 will help you to distinguish between the experiences of stress, overwhelm and homeostasis.

Let's get going!

PART I

KNOW

CHAPTER 1

REALISE YOUR REALITY

'There are no death camps in corporations,
but many apparently successful companies
hide great suffering in their basements.'

– FRED KOFMAN

T he 1994 movie *The Shawshank Redemption* is praised as the
greatest film never to win an Oscar. The film, starring Tim
Robbins (portraying Andy Dufresne) and Morgan Freeman
(portraying Red), tells the story of a twenty-year relationship
between two inmates at Shawshank State Penitentiary. Andy and
Red share their unique stories of the harrowing conditions, both
physical and mental, and the psyche required to withstand life
inside the prison. Through the trials and tribulations, we come
to learn from Andy that his greatest motivators of endurance are
hope and purpose greater than oneself.

As Andy says, *'There are places in this world that aren't made out
of stone... there's something inside... that they can't get to, that they
can't touch. That's yours... Hope.'* It is hope that motivates Andy
to smuggle in a rock hammer and a poster of Rita Hayworth,
and then go on to tunnel through the prison walls – a task that

took nineteen years of commitment and consistency before Andy realised his goal of freedom.

By the end of the film, we also see Red's story of transformation unfold. From feeling institutionalised:

'*These walls are funny. First you hate 'em. Then you get used to 'em. Enough time passes, you get so you depend on them. That's institutionalised.*'

... to being in control and taking action:

'*I guess it comes down to a simple choice, really. Get busy living or get busy dying.*'

Right now, you probably feel more hopeless than hopeful. I've been there, too, and know it is an absolute punishment. So, let's have a look at a few of the reasons why initiating and managing change at work has become such a joy thief in your life. Let's start with some simple metaphors, inspired by *The Shawshank Redemption*.

TRAPPED LIKE A PRISONER

In a hyper-competitive VUCA (volatile, uncertain, complex and ambiguous) world, change is touted as a constant opportunity for organisations to digitally transform, innovate and create new value offerings for clients. But in your mind, the high volume of change you are experiencing has left you exhausted, overwhelmed and hyper-anxious. Your reality is closer to one of a prison inmate, like Andy and Red in *The Shawshank Redemption*. Continuing with that metaphor, here are some other notions you may relate to:

RESISTING ARREST

'But I didn't ask for this extra workload or change responsibility – it was pushed down from above.' Your cries for support have fallen on deaf ears. And the advice from those who have gone before you is that the house always wins where resistance and resources are concerned.

LIFE SENTENCE

The judge has ruled in favour of 'change as usual' (CAU). The rapid pace of change is forever set in motion. You instantly freeze and switch from thriving mode to surviving mode. This activates a constant state of uncertainty, anxiety and fear. It is clear you lack the suitable coping mechanisms.

GOLDEN HANDCUFFS

With lock-up comes jewellery. Golden handcuffs ensure you endure the change chaos taking place around you. Golden hand-cuffs represent your salary or annual bonus, which keeps you at the mercy of a stressful job or toxic boss. Like others, you have a mortgage to pay off and family responsibilities. It's time to focus on 'getting shit done'.

PRISONISATION

This is the point where you no longer resist your reality. Over time, you've had to learn to adapt. Your once independent nature is now co-dependent on cultural norms, espoused values and groupthink. There are downsides to being institutionalised. You are guarded, distrusting of others and emotionally numb.

THE USUAL SUSPECTS

In the change failure slammer, you'll find a variety of social misfits. Overworked, overstretched and overwhelmed. They relentlessly shadow you day and night, always watching and always baiting you. This isn't the kind of social support and community spirit you had anticipated.

TOP DOG

Then there is the infamous top dog or number one. The leader always sets the tone from the top, often sharing need-to-know information just in time. Don't cross the leader – you would do well to appease him or her. When under pressure, most of them are binary in their decision making. They view others as 'capable' or 'incapable' of getting the job done.

SOLITARY CONFINEMENT

When trust is absent among cell mates, it can be incredibly isolating. You keep your head low and your mouth shut. At night, you lie awake thinking about worst-case scenarios. You know you should be sleeping, but you are too edgy.

THE GREAT ESCAPE

Out of desperation, you hatch a plan to tunnel your way out. It's a slow and considered strategy, because you have to line a few things up before you have the confidence to actually do it. Hope is the only thing keeping you going now. You file an application for your sabbatical or write your resignation and slip away in the darkness.

These metaphors are designed to help you reflect on your situation. Here, the starkness of the inner mental prison is designed to highlight the intensity of your subjective emotional experience. Emotions are so often overlooked or labelled as irrelevant – or even detrimental – in the workplace. Most workplaces condition you to hide them, even though this is at odds with the very nature of being human. However, 'prison talk' is probably not the type of language that is going to assist you in having a meaningful conversation with your team, your boss or Human Resources!

In the workplace, models remain the preferred communication tool for reframing ideas and sharing narratives. So, I have created a model that is designed to provide you with workplace-appropriate language to help you articulate exactly where you are at and what you are experiencing. Of course, this language isn't just reserved for conversations with others. You can use it internally, too, to help you better understand your relationship with change.

THE HUMAN STATES OF CHANGE

Having worked on all sides of change, both being on the receiving end of it (change target) and being responsible for leading large teams (change lead), what I have observed are eight common Human Change States, which influence your personal relationship with change. These are:

- Change Oblivious
- Change Bravado
- Change Anxiety
- Change Resistance
- Change Capable
- Change Frustration

- Change Fatigue
- Change Burnout

Let's look at the Human Change State (HCS) model more closely so that you can assess where you are at (your current reality) and determine where you want to shift to (your desired future).

Figure 3 illustrates the eight Human Change States, based on which 'zone' they belong to (more on this in a minute). These states are not fixed or linear due to the complexity associated with change. In fact, certain change scenarios (such as redundancies, restructuring or resilience upskilling) will cause you to oscillate between the different change states. However, for the most part, you will have a dominant Human Change State that you are currently operating from.

Figure 3: Human change states.
Adapted from Tom Senninger's Learning Zone Model, expanded from Lev Vygotsky's Zone of Proximal Development.

STATUS QUO ZONE

In the twenty-first century, organisations and individuals that operate from within the status quo are the greatest enemies of progress. Creativity, collaboration and innovation cannot flourish in these conditions. The status quo zone is home to the first two Human Change States: Change Oblivious and Change Bravado.

1. Change Oblivious

Change Oblivious is when you are comfortable with having no, or very limited, awareness and knowledge about change in general. Another way of describing being blissfully unaware is 'ostriching' because others may perceive you as having your head in the sand. Your focus is elsewhere and you don't seem to care.

2. Change Bravado

This second state is where you are aware of, but don't care about, the changes taking place around you. This is a more outwardly confident position that is often referred to as 'peacocking'. Others may perceive you as being overly secure and egotistical. It is obvious that your focus is not on the change taking place. Internally, though, you intuitively know you are hiding behind this false confidence as an avoidance strategy.

OVERWHELM ZONE

In both work and life, fear tends to creep up on you in subtle ways. These subtleties cumulate and compound, surfacing in various implicit and explicit forms. The overwhelm zone is where Change Anxiety (implicit form) and Change Resistance (explicit form) reside.

3. Change Anxiety

The third state is where you feel worried and fearful about change specifics or change as a general topic. Both the known and unknown details can result in Change Anxiety. In other words, you worry about information that has been shared. Then you start questioning missing information and often fill in the gaps with assumptions. These assumptions tend to skew towards catastrophising extremes. This is where you default to worst-case scenarios. While this is a primal instinct intended to keep you safe from danger, Change Anxiety is also reflective of a lack of self-confidence and self-worth.

4. Change Resistance

The fourth state is the most commonly discussed and documented term. Change Resistance refers to a state of opposition towards either the change itself or the individuals or leadership team acting as the driving force. It is usually a high-energy, negative state. Those with higher emotional intelligence would self-describe as 'being passionate and constructive', while those with a blind spot are more likely to be labelled by others as 'defensive and change resistant'. This is often viewed as career-limiting behaviour.

GROWTH ZONE

Personal growth can only occur when you leave the status quo zone. It is a fluid state where you stretch and grow through learning and experiences. The growth zone is sustainable when the level of personal stress falls within the optimal range of your 'allostatic load'. This refers to the impact of stress or the 'wear and tear' on your body. In a state of stress, your body mines energy from elsewhere in the body to allow you to adapt and function in the present. However, if it is repeatedly overloaded, the body will eventually crash, seeking regeneration.

5. Change Capable

The fifth state is the peak state of growth where you are resilient, ready and resourceful in relation to change. If you are not resourceful, then you fall back into either Change Resistance or Change Anxiety. When in the Change Capable state, you embody a sense of hope, real optimism and authentic confidence. You feel supported, connected, informed and upskilled. Without any reservation, you prioritise personal and professional growth over stagnation.

6. Change Frustration

The sixth state refers to your annoyance at the pace of change. From your perspective, it is either too slow or too fast. Frustration is often viewed as a negative. However, this is an important state as it shows that you still have a high level of care for and investment in the change. Nurturing is much more manageable from the Change Frustration state than from the Change Fatigue state. This is usually where the biggest missed opportunities occur in organisations.

BURNOUT ZONE

Nothing good comes from the burnout zone. Trust, respect and connection are in rapid decline, and you feel at odds or misaligned with the organisation's purpose, values and transformation direction. Your brain, mind and body experience the impact of psychological warfare. This will be explored in greater detail later in the book.

7. Change Fatigue

The seventh state elicits physical and mental tiredness as well as a decline in energetic enthusiasm. Take caution. The expression 'change fatigue' should not be taken lightly. If this term is commonplace in your organisation, your team or your own vernacular, then you need to shake yourself out of complacency and be on high alert. Change Fatigue is a precursor to change overload and eventual burnout. And what is most concerning is that, much like a health diagnosis, there is no definitive time frame for how quickly your personal fuse will break or melt.

8. Change Burnout

The eighth state is the point of no return. The high velocity and compounding impact of exponential work/life change has overpowered you to the point of job burnout. This is vastly different to being tired after a day's work or one bad night's sleep. Burnout is with you twenty-four hours until it is addressed.

PAUSE & REFLECT

- Which of the eight Human Change States do you relate most to and why?
- Would others agree with your self-assessment?
- Do you believe that the Human Change State that you are currently operating from is best serving you and your future self?
- Is there another Human Change State that would set you up for success?

(Hint: It's becoming Change Capable.)

With regard to the eighth state, Change Burnout, sometimes it isn't always obvious that you are actually in this state – simply because you're so strung out and simply trying to get through each day. In the following section, I'll explain how to recognise when you've reached Change Burnout.

CRASH AND BURN

Close your eyes and imagine blowing out a candle. That unique smell floods your nostrils and you are captivated by the trance-like dance of the smoke moving upwards. And then *click* – in an instant, it's gone. Light one minute, dark the next. This is what burnout can feel like. It can creep up on you – until one day you suddenly crash. The only way to avoid a crash is to address burnout as soon as you recognise it. Figure 4 provides a snapshot of how you recognise when burnout is present in you:

Figure 4: Crash & Burn.

You are drowning
You are experiencing:

- Exhaustion beyond chronic stress (physical, mental and emotional exhaustion)

- Sleep disturbance, including rumination and insomnia
- Cognitive impairment to judgement, decision making and memory retrieval

You are disengaged
You are feeling:

- Under-challenged yet overloaded with work
- Depersonalisation, as shown by your lack of care and concern for your work
- A tendency to default to critical, cynical or apathetic responses

You are discouraged
You are experiencing:

- A lack of professional efficacy (the positive feelings associated with job competency)
- Low autonomy or low recognition
- Isolation as a result of low social connection or out-grouping

In human burnout, as opposed to candle burnout, the smoke spirals downwards rather than up. Indeed, the spiral of descent can be so rapid that it feels uncontrollable. There is a distinct point of no return, a letting go, when you simply succumb to the exhaustion. You are physically and mentally incapable of fighting on the front foot, defending on the back foot or withstanding any form of conflict whatsoever. You are a broken soul and the shame of being found so fractionated consumes you.

Ripples beyond work include insomnia, lowered immunity, physical illness, marital strain and relationship pressures, leading to mental health challenges, such as anxiety and depression, and even suicide.

For the remainder of the book, I will interchangeably refer to the terms 'overload', 'fatigue' and 'burnout', which encompass the following symptoms:

CHANGE OVERLOAD AND BURNOUT SYMPTOMS

Cognitive

- Irritability (defensive/ hyper-sensitive)
- Poor decision making (clouded judgement/ memory concerns)
- Rigid thinking (absence of creative/critical thinking)

Emotional

- Emotion-full to emotion-less (human being to corporate robot)
- Spiralling (frustration to anger to apathy)
- Learned helplessness (lacking hope)

Behavioural

- Sleep irregularities (ruminating and waking at 2am)
- Increased isolation (seeking refuge via withdrawal)
- Presenteeism followed by absenteeism

Physical

- Exhaustion (apparent at the start of the day)
- Stress symptoms (change in heart rate and breathing)
- Lowered immune system (resulting in more general ailments)

Personality

- Type A skewed (ambitious workaholics)
- Perfectionist (mistrusting and controlling)
- Vice seeking (alcohol, drugs, smoking, shopping, screen time and people pleasing)

Spiritual

- Loss of purpose (the cause that inspires you)
- Diminished sense of career enjoyment
- Questioning spirituality and quality of relationships

Being expected to thrive in times of uncertainty and change is no easy feat. If it were, you would be thriving in your job and excited about the future.

Change used to be exciting and bring with it great promise. However, right now, change is having the opposite effect. If you are currently experiencing any of the symptoms outlined in the table, then my heart goes out to you. It is not a good place to be in, even if temporary.

Remember that my role is not to enable or empower you. That would be very self-righteous of me. Instead, I want you to liberate yourself. So, I will provide you with a variety of methods and insights for you to test out and see what works for you. Conscious awareness provides you with the ability to navigate your own unique journey at a pace and tone that aligns with what you need to *hear*, *feel* and *experience* in that moment.

ALL IT TAKES IS PRESSURE AND TIME

Psychologist Herbert Freudenberger is thought to have conducted the first piece of burnout research in 1974. However, only as recently as 2019 has the World Health Organization (WHO) declared that burnout is a 'workplace syndrome'. This suggests that more research and preventative measures will arise in the future.

A 2019 study from Kronos, published by *Forbes*, identified that key burnout indicators could be attributed to poor management (thirty per cent), employees not seeing how their role connects to corporate strategy (twenty-nine per cent), and a negative work-place culture (twenty-six per cent). This study highlights the fact that organisations, teams and individuals must all be held accountable for the rise in burnout. Collective sponsorship, action and measures should be prioritised to prevent it from becoming a twenty-first century epidemic.

The American Psychological Association's (APA) 2017 Work and Well-Being Survey of 1,500 workers found that leadership often underestimates the impact that organisational changes have on employees:

'Workers experiencing recent or current change were more than twice as likely to report chronic work stress compared with employees who reported no recent, current or anticipated change (55 percent vs. 22 percent), and more than four times as likely to report experiencing physical health symptoms at work (34 percent vs. 8 percent).

'Working Americans who reported recent or current change were more likely to say they experienced work-life conflict (39 percent vs. 12 percent for job interfering with non-work responsibilities and 32 percent vs. 7 percent for home and family responsibilities interfering with work), [and] felt cynical and negative toward others during the workday (35 percent vs. 11 percent)...

'For organisations to successfully navigate turbulent times, they need resilient employees who can adapt to change... To build trust and engagement, employers need to focus on building a psychologically healthy workplace where employees are

actively involved in shaping the future and confident in their ability to succeed.'

Brent Gleeson, in a *Forbes* article titled '1 Reason Why Most Change Management Efforts Fail', writes:

'Change battle fatigue is the result of many elements such as past failures plaguing the minds of employees and the sacrifices made during the arduous change process. When a transformation is poorly led, fatigue can set in quickly. And not only do 70% of organisational transformations fail, but that failure rate may even be increasing. According to 2008 research from IBM, the need to lead change is growing, but our ability to do it is shrinking. Hence why people often get discouraged and eventually give up.'

In a TEDx Talk titled 'Burnout and post-traumatic stress disorder', Dr. Geri Puleo shared her PhD research on burnout due to organisational change, stating, *'The similarities between burnout and Post Traumatic Stress, PTSD, are shocking. In fact, I'm a firm believer that burnout is a form of PTSD.'*

Similarities include a decline in health, personal relationships turning sour, fear and hopelessness responses, depression and withdrawal, irritability and mood changes, residual burnout where you re-live the experience, and so on.

Dr. Puleo's research shows the descent down to burnout, due to organisational change, takes an average of six months for change targets and one to two years for change leaders. Meanwhile, the ascent out of burnout, or the recovery phase, averages two years, meaning that it takes longer for the individual to feel 'whole' again.

Dr. Puleo's research argues that poor leadership and lack of organisational caring easily outranks work overload as the leading cause of burnout. 'Organisational caring' can be defined as a structure of values and organising principles centred on fulfilling employees' needs, promoting employees' best interests and valuing employees' contributions. Is this a unicorn term or have you experienced this firsthand? If you are reading this book, I'm guessing not.

In a *Harvard Business Review* article titled 'Employee Burnout Is a Problem with the Company, Not the Person', Eric Garton argues:

> 'Executives need to own up to their role in creating the workplace stress that leads to burnout... Unchecked organisational norms insidiously create the conditions for burnout—but leaders can change them to make burnout less likely.'

You may have been advised that how you approach and handle workplace change will better position you for your next career leap or more generally for the future of work. This is the equivalent of telling graduate intakes that they are 'special', or the 'chosen ones', to anchor a baseline of fear within them, so that they don't fall below a certain threshold of standards.

This is a call to arms that we all need to get better at recognising and expressing emotions in ourselves and others. Labelling the Human Change States associated with change overload and burnout is only the tip of the iceberg.

This new knowledge will also act as a roadmap towards empathy and compassion. To better understand how others around you experience human suffering. It can assist you in commencing coaching conversations with others who are having a tough time coping with change. Remember that role-modelling more human qualities will be regarded as a strength in the future workplace – one that should be spotlighted and not ignored or minimised.

THE DANGER OF EMOTIONAL CONTAGION

Emotions are often defined as *energy in motion*. They are more powerful than most people give them credit for. They range from joyful and constructive to fear-inducing and destructive. Your emotional data and emotions themselves are always being transmitted.

Emotional contagion is when a person or group's emotions trigger similar emotions, moods and behaviours in another person or group. Through subconscious processing of facial expressions, vocal tone and other readable body language, the person or group 'catches' and 'mimics' the emotions that are energetically charging the environment. Specifically, your subconscious mind is always noticing, interpreting and predicting what is taking place around you. This refers to the full spectrum of emotions, including joy, anger and distress.

In the book *Contagious You*, author Anese Cavanaugh states, *'Your Contagion Factor is how contagious you are, how far it will ripple, how positively or negatively so, and how likely you'll then be to create the result you want.'*

From an evolutionary psychology perspective, mirror neurons ensured you had the ability to connect with others and connect with the tribe at large. You see, back in tribal days, we were not self-sustaining and needed the tribe to keep us safe from enemies. From a neuroscientific perspective, it is the mirror neurons in our brain that enable 'catching' or 'mirroring'. Mirror neurons fire even when they are orchestrating and not doing an action. In an article titled 'Do Mirror Neurons Give Us Empathy?' Vilayanur Ramachandran, professor of neuroscience at the University of California, states:

> 'A subset of these neurons also fire when I simply watch another person—watch you reach out and do exactly the same action. So, these neurons are performing a virtual reality simulation of your mind, your brain. Therefore, they're constructing a theory of your mind—of your intention—which is important for all kinds of social interaction.'

Ramachandran goes on to use the example of how anterior cingulate neurons fire when he pokes his thumb with a needle:

> 'It turns out these anterior cingulate neurons that respond to my thumb being poked will also fire when I watch you being poked—but only a subset of them. There are non-mirror neuron pain neurons and there are mirror neuron pain neurons.

> 'So, these [mirror] neurons are probably involved in empathy for pain. If I really and truly empathise with your pain, I need to experience it myself. That's what the mirror neurons are doing, allowing me to empathise with your pain—saying,

in effect, that person is experiencing the same agony and excruciating pain as you would if somebody were to poke you with a needle directly. That's the basis of all empathy.'

Note that while emotional contagion is one of many elements of empathy, it is not empathy in its entirety. Empathy is a choice to engage in while emotional contagion is an automatic response. More like a fast, reflective action.

The implications of emotional contagion influence your mental wellbeing. For example, if your leaders are not making tough people calls, and taking a stand on culture as part of business transformation and organisational change efforts, then leave. Emotional contagion confirms that no matter how much personal development work you do, you will still be at risk of snapping back and undoing all your efforts when you re-enter a dysfunctional culture.

In a *Psychology Today* article titled 'Protect Yourself from Emotional Contagion', Elaine Hatfield, co-author of the pioneering, academic book *Emotional Contagion* and a professor of psychology at the University of Hawaii, stated:

'Repeatedly catching negative emotions from the people in our lives can create a miasma – preventing us from seeing the contagion or its cause. Instead, we sense we're in an unhealthy environment. And in worst-case scenarios, emotional contagion leads to harmful actions.'

PAUSE & REFLECT

- Have you experienced emotional contagion firsthand?
- Was it a positive or negative experience?
- Was it short-lived or long-lasting?
- Can you pinpoint major contributors?
- Being honest with yourself, have you ever been the instigator?

Workplace stress is nothing new. However, what is concerning is the speed with which stress is being replaced by the spread of emotional contagion and burnout.

REACHING OUT MATTERS

When change overload and burnout are ignored or minimised, there can be mental health repercussions. Should you be concerned about your mental health or have a diagnosable clinical disorder, please seek professional help from your GP.

Reimagine Change is not intended to be a substitute for professional medical advice, diagnosis or treatment. Always refer to a mental health professional or other qualified health provider with any questions you may have. The following contacts have been sourced from Healthdirect Australia, a national, government-owned, not-for-profit organisation.

Lifeline provides twenty-four-hour crisis counselling, support groups and suicide prevention services. Call 13 11 14.

Suicide Call Back Service provides twenty-four-hour, seven-days-a-week support if you or someone you know is feeling suicidal. Call 1300 659 467.

Beyond Blue aims to increase awareness of depression and anxiety, and reduce stigma. Call 1300 22 46 36.

MensLine Australia is a professional telephone and online support and information service for Australian men. Call 1300 789 978.

MindSpot is a free telephone and online assessment service for people with stress, worry, anxiety, low mood or depression. Mind-Spot is not an emergency or instant response service. Call 1800 614 434.

SANE Australia provides support, training and education, enabling those with a mental illness to lead a better life. Call 1800 187 263.

CHAPTER SUMMARY

That brings us to the end of Chapter 1. By now, you should have gathered some valuable insights and data to help you realise that what you are seeing, feeling and experiencing is not unique to you. Unfortunately, it is more commonplace than most individuals and organisations imagine.

In Chapter 2, we'll discuss how to shift from 'Now that I know' to 'What am I going to do about it?' and 'Why would that be of value to me?' Before we dive into that, let's review the key points discussed in Chapter 1:

- There are eight Human Change States that aspiring change leaders can experience:
    > Change Oblivious
    > Change Bravado
    > Change Anxiety
    > Change Resistance
    > Change Capable
    > Change Frustration
    > Change Fatigue
    > Change Burnout

- Addressing change fatigue is increasingly important. When left unaddressed, an individual's change capacity or change bandwidth will eventually reach a tipping point.

- Research shows the descent down to burnout, due to organisational change, takes an average of six months for change targets (those impacted by change) and one to two years for change leaders (those leading change efforts).

• Recognise the onset of burnout starts with three lead indicators – you are drowning, disengaged and discouraged. Don't ignore these indicators during difficult times.

• Thanks to the mirror neurons in your brain, emotional contagion is a contributing factor to triggering and retriggering change fatigue and burnout in individuals and teams.

• When change overload and burnout are ignored or minimised, this can significantly impact your mental health. For mental health support, including a referral to a mental health profes-sional, please speak to your GP.

CHAPTER 2

RESPOND VIA YOUR CAPABILITY

*'When we are no longer able to change a situation, we
are challenged to change ourselves.'*

– VIKTOR FRANKL

n Steven Spielberg's 2002 thriller *Catch Me If You Can*, central
character Frank Abagnale (played by Leonardo DiCaprio) is
the youngest person ever to make the FBI's Ten Most Wanted
Fugitives in the 1960s. After running away from home at age sixteen, Abagnale becomes a self-made con artist with a panache for
forging bank cheques ($4 million worth!) and impersonating an
airline pilot, a doctor and a lawyer.

Over many years, Frank Abagnale is pursued by FBI agent Carl
Hanratty (Tom Hanks) and this becomes a pseudo parental relationship in the absence of approval from Frank's real father, also
a low-scale con artist, Abagnale Senior (played by Christopher
Walken). Throughout the movie, Abagnale Junior repeats a mantra,
one that he originally listened to his father tell at an awards cer-
emony. It goes like this:

'Two little mice fell in a bucket of cream. The first mouse quickly gave up and drowned. The second mouse wouldn't quit. He struggled so hard that eventually he churned that cream into butter and crawled out. Gentlemen, as of this moment, I am that second mouse.'

Here, the bucket of cream is a metaphor for life's success. It implies that few people stumble upon success or have it handed to them. Most will have to pursue it. This is often akin to a journey or series of trials and tribulations that need to be overcome. However, for those that are willing to invest in the required work and push through the fear zone, both the learning experience and payoff will be rewarding.

PAUSE & REFLECT

- Which mouse best represents you? The quitter or the opportunist?
- What choices are you making? Are you predisposed to drown in the status quo? Or are you mustering up strength to make your next move?
- Will you permit change overload and burnout to rob you of mental strength and wellness, or will you fight back?

Regardless of the situation you find yourself in, you always have a choice as to how you respond. In this chapter, we'll focus on the value of self-mobilised change capability. Before you attempt to get any traction, you need to call time on your antagonists (also known as your handbrakes) and call in your allies (also known as your accelerators). Let's explore that now.

CALL TIME ON YOUR ANTAGONISTS

Most of us think that better choices come from doing more. Quite the opposite. Traction yields from the art of doing less. In the book *What Got You Here Won't Get You There*, author Marshall Goldsmith says:

> 'We spend a lot of time teaching leaders what to do. We don't spend enough time teaching leaders what to stop. Half the leaders I have met don't need to learn what to do. They need to learn what to stop.'

To effectively respond, you may need to stop before you drop. When I say 'drop', I mean drop down into despair, hopelessness, apathy and so on. Down there, you are no good to anyone. So, if you value your career, your relationships and your future potential, you are going to need to shift your mindset. This is self-sustainability at its core.

First up, let's look at a few of the more common 'state of mind' antagonists that may be standing in your way of making better choices. The antagonists of overcoming change overload and burnout are:

- Avoiding your reality
- Masking your emotions
- Attaching via co-dependency

- Shaming oneself
- Blaming external forces
- Isolating from connection

I. AVOIDING YOUR REALITY

This is when you are willingly ignoring the reality of what is taking place around you. Complacency and procrastination are two classic avoidance tactics. This indecisiveness is designed to keep you feeling safe. And when you want to feel safe, you default to your comfort zone, your self-serving bias and your autopilot thinking.

The comfort zone

This is a psychological state where you feel safe and in control. The environment is familiar to you and you feel at ease in it due to having a perceived level of control. Sub-optimal performance resides here and you have established that this does not bring you discomfort.

Self-serving bias

This is a cognitive bias, studied in social psychology, which is designed to preserve your self-esteem and ego. When positive outcomes occur, you take full credit. But when negative outcomes occur, you are quick to extend the blame externally.

Autopilot thinking

This is when you 'switch off' and allow your mind to wander. When this is taking place, research has shown that a continuous stream of unconscious activity still registers. For example, your mind constantly runs through future predictions in an attempt to keep you feeling safe from harm.

2. MASKING YOUR EMOTIONS

Founder of Jungian psychology Carl Jung coined the term 'persona' in relation to those who wear different (invisible) masks for different social groups or situations. Jung described a persona as *'a kind of mask, designed on the one hand to make a definite impression upon others, and on the other to conceal the true nature of the individual'.* Two common corporate personas or masks are:

Charismatic leader

You lead with bravado and ego. Like a gambler, you talk up the wins but never the losses. Inside your mind, you cannot reach out for help without being found out. According to organisational psychologist Tomas Chamorro-Premuzic, *'one of the best ways to fool other people into thinking that you're better than you actually are is to fool yourself first.'*

Corporate robot

You are ultra-professional to the extent that you are emotionless. It keeps you safe from possibly leaking information that will make you look weak in front of colleagues. You wrongly believe people respect you for this. They don't.

Any form of masking erodes self-alignment and commonly leads to the onset of imposter syndrome. This is where you wrestle with the prospect of being uniquely you. Masking and subsequent de-masking are huge energy thieves, particularly when it comes to your future self versus your present self. In her book *The Willpower Instinct*, psychologist Kelly McGonigal explains, *'We think about our future selves like different people. We often idealise them, expecting our future selves to do what our present selves cannot manage.'*

3. ATTACHING VIA CO-DEPENDENCY

This is when you are co-dependent on your work, workplace relationships and workplace purpose. You have given all of your independent power to those around you. You are most likely an empath who absorbs others' emotions. Be aware that co-dependency is linked to self-worth issues. This will be explored in future chapters.

Workaholism is a type of co-dependency. You aren't worried about being retrenched; you already are the ultimate co-bot. One who is extremely conscientious, takes on any and all new requests, and is an integral, go-to member of the team. You live and breathe the work, and pander to others' needs in the hope that your people pleasing will be revered.

However, when anxious attachment needs aren't met, the subconscious seeks out destruction elsewhere. This is when you reach for vices as an outlet, or as an escape from the reality of endless expectations and worries. Vices may be in the form of alcohol, drugs, sex, food, shopping, social media, video games, television marathons and so on. The spiritual implication is one of unfulfillment and a deep lack of self-love. Often, what you'll find is that the root cause stems from either childhood or workplace trauma.

4. SHAMING ONESELF

Here, shame refers to the internalising of self-blame, where you give yourself a hard time if you have failed at something. Self-judgement and inner-critic conversations start off innocently before becoming all-consuming. Thanks to negative self-talk, you'll eventually be asking yourself: How have I let things get this bad? Other words that are associated with shame are inadequacy, insecurity and worthlessness.

One of the more challenging sides of shame is when your personal values have been violated and repression sets in as a way of self-soothing the mind. Reverting to vices as a coping mechanism is another common side effect of shame. In an *Inc.* article titled 'Brene Brown on How to Avoid a Perfect Shame Spiral at Work', author Ilan Mochari writes:

> *'In business settings, these voids of non-communication happen all the time. What matters, in these cases, is that someone on your team is brave enough, vulnerable enough, to use a sentence that starts with, "The story I'm making up right now is..." The idea is to reach the truth as quickly as possible, instead of wandering around with your made-up explanation, which more than likely consists of your own shame triggers, and has little relation to reality.'*

5. BLAMING EXTERNAL FORCES

This is an extension of self-serving bias, outlined earlier. Blaming is the potent combination of anger, resentment, resistance and underlying fear. It is the fear of not being included, heard, valued and appreciated. It is the transference of being blamed in the past. It is the distorting of a situation so that you do not take on more blame yourself. All of these result in a victim mindset.

Delusions of self-confidence manifest as blaming, too. While such delusions can help you to achieve, they can also make it difficult for you to change. In fact, when others suggest that it is you who needs to change, you may respond with unadulterated bafflement.

Blaming is as much a declaration of independence as it is a cry for help over recent adversities. This often goes unresolved as co-workers and loved ones are met with a prickly response when they try to approach you for a calm discussion. Your irritable mood flares up and sets the tone for the rest of the day. When blaming is active, self-awareness has left the building.

6. ISOLATING FROM CONNECTION

This is more prevalent than ever in light of the global pandemic crisis, COVID-19, and the subsequent need to quarantine and self-isolate. For many, the psychological impact of cabin fever, solitary confinement and global uncertainty was anxiety on an unprecedented level.

As mammals, our innate nature is to care for and nurture each other. In these times, the sense of touch was taken away from us – no hand shaking, touching or hugging. For so many people who live alone or far from family, this was exacerbated. The physical workplace is no different.

In a *Harvard Business Review* article titled 'The Surprising Power of Simply Asking Coworkers How They're Doing', Karyn Twaronite points to the EY Belonging Barometer study, which surveyed 1,000 employed American adults and found 'exclusion is a growing issue'. The article states, '*We found that more than 40% of those surveyed are feeling physically and emotionally isolated in the workplace.*'

Checking in in person, and asking others about their work and personal lives, was deemed by survey participants to be far more important than other senior leadership activities such as inclusion on emails, invites to events or surface-level work conversations.

CALL IN YOUR ALLIES

In the absence of organisational or leadership action, you need to self-mobilise and upskill in change capability to reinstate your potential and thrive. Don't worry – I'm not going to balance out the six antagonists with six allies. Let's just focus on three. After all, good things come in threes!

Your three key allies to overcoming change overload and burnout are:

- Self-awareness
- Self-accountability
- Self-mobilisation

Yes, yes – I know what you are thinking. 'But our organisational values are hinged upon the likes of contribution, collaboration and creativity.' That's all well and good in theory. But the reality is that until you do the inner work, your contribution to collaborative work is going to be sub-optimal. It is going to be tainted with psychological restraints such as blame, resentment and exhaustion. You see, when you're functioning from a place of survival, you'll struggle to find the necessary courage, creativity and flow.

Most leaders have risen from the ranks of being labelled top talent or star performers. The impact of this is that the desire and ability to lead and coach teams is usually less than the desire for the egotistical gain of status and salary. This perpetuates a vicious cycle of leaders lacking human-centred skills and leadership qualities such as empathy, energy management and optimism.

This is not a beat down. We have all forged our way in the world, using the learnings (the good, the bad and the ugly) that we have absorbed from our parents, school, university, social networks and workplaces. Role models are never assigned but they are ever-present. Every person you are exposed to plays a role. However, there is a point in your life where you cannot rely on others to fuel your belief and motivation; it must be self-derived for you to expand, energise and illuminate.

So, let's now explore each of these allies individually.

I. SELF-AWARENESS

Think you're self-aware? Think again. The truth of the matter is that most of us don't know our true selves. We go through our daily lives with the false belief that we are already self-aware. (Guilty as charged!)

Tasha Eurich, organisational psychologist and author of *Insight: The Power of Self-Awareness in a Self-Deluded World*, is the global thought leader on self-awareness. Her research shows that most of us are, in fact, not self-aware at all. According to Eurich, *'95% of people think they're self-aware, but the real number is closer to 10% to 15%.'* This is particularly problematic in the context of leadership. Eurich states, *'You can't have a self-aware organisation if the most visible and influential leader is, for lack of a better word, delusional.'*

If most of us are delusional (according to Eurich), then let's explore what real self-awareness looks like. When self-awareness is activated, you are able to observe whether your thoughts and behaviours align with both the workplace cultural context and the inner standards that you measure yourself against. The two sub-types of self-awareness are:

- **Internal self-awareness:** Where you are aware of your personal strengths and values, and how they fit your environment and impact others. This results in work/life alignment, greater social satisfaction and overall happiness.

- **External self-awareness:** Where you are aware of how others view your leadership. This results in you choosing to be more empathic to the needs of your team, with an emphasis on relationship building. You are attuned to moods and dynamics shifting, and seek to understand and rectify the situation.

When learning about self-awareness, you need to also be aware of the psychological term 'cognitive dissonance'. This refers to the inner disharmony of your beliefs and values, to the extent that you will defend them even when they are proven wrong. Common mismatches include identifying as a smoker, even though you are aware of the negative health implications.

Another example is the belief that you are upholding cultural norms ('That's not the way we do things around here'), even though new process improvements have been tested and validated as a clear improvement to workflow. To move forward from that stance, you have to either acquire new information, lessen your belief or change your belief altogether to reduce the inner disharmony.

Eurich provides three key tips to build self-awareness:

- **Be braver but wiser:** Make the decision that you want to know the truth.
- **Embrace objectivity from others:** Ask for feedback.
- **Shift out of self-critique:** Ask 'what', not 'why', questions.

Three key values that can be extracted from this are integrity, authenticity and intentional action. Integrity is not an idea designed to be plastered on a motivational poster; it is a value that you intrinsically cultivate by choice, not coercion. Authenticity is not to be demanded by or from another; it needs to be fostered in psychologically safe environments where others display it rather than demand it. Intentional action is not found on Kanban boards. It keeps you moving through your day with purpose, passion and positivity.

All of these start with you. Most people are waiting for signs and symbols of when and how to take action. Yet, these three values alone can act as your compass as you continue on to *Reimagine Change*. These three values are the foundation of liberation. The process to make this a reality is self-directed coaching. This involves tapping into your intuition to find the answers that are right for you. One of the most effective ways to do this is through the practice of journaling. (More about this in future chapters.)

2. SELF-ACCOUNTABILITY

Think self-accountability is a given? Think again. Self-accountability is steeped in integrity and infused with credibility, consistency and congruent choices. You are clear on your responsibilities and follow through. You are able to bridge the gap between motivation and momentum all by yourself.

PAUSE & REFLECT

- Do you identify as someone who follows through, executes and achieves? Or are you more likely to shirk self-responsibility?
- If it's the latter, do you cover it up or proactively own it?

The key difference between people who follow through, execute and achieve and those who do not is radical self-accountability (RSA). In the future of work, more self-organising teams will be prevalent. These will demand knowledge around change philosophies and attitudes. You will be expected to take care of yourself and your team. How does that sit with you, given your personal track record?

3. SELF-MOBILISATION

Within organisations, we see either limited or passive participation in change initiatives. More recently, there has been a positive trend towards co-creation. This is where change targets and change leaders are invited to actively contribute to the design, testing and deployment of change initiatives. Working shoulder to shoulder with the consultants or internal transformation teams reframes change from being 'done *to* them' to being 'done *with* them'. This promotes buy-in and increased access to resources.

Self-mobilisation differs to co-creation in that it can take place at the individual or community level. This is where you or your community take on change initiatives or change-related upskilling, external to the organisation where you work. This relies on the belief that individuals are capable of self-reviewing their current change predicament and being the driving force to implement change themselves.

If you have been entrenched in a hierarchical organisation, you are at risk of being or becoming a co-dependent follower. It's time to take charge of your own personal development. You can't be expected to develop others if you haven't been developing yourself. Self-mobilisation is the antithesis of feeling stuck. It is the opposite of inaction. It is the intrinsic drive behind the mindset of 'think it, feel it, believe it, stick with it and, most importantly, get it done'.

FROM CHANGE SURVIVOR TO CHANGE OPTIMISER

Change capability is critical to your success. There are six levels of change capability, defined as Milestone Identities, as shown in Figure 5: 'Lead the change'.

Figure 5 illustrates the identity shift from Change Survivor to Change Optimiser, where you will begin to *state shift* from being a replaceable commodity to a leading asset.

Before looking at each of the Milestone Identities, let me quickly outline what I mean by sub-optimal versus optimal in the context of change capability.

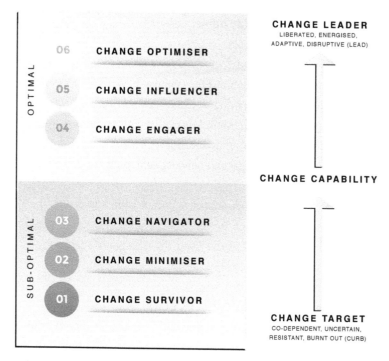

Figure 5: Lead the change.

Sub-optimal change capability domains:

- Interpersonal: Masking and imposter syndrome
- Physical: Exhausted, especially first thing in the morning
- Emotional: Fear and anxiety-based coping responses
- Intellectual: Brain fog and internalisation
- Social: Avoidance and isolation
- Occupational: Disengaged and unappreciated
- Spiritual: Unfulfilled, lacking self-love, as evidenced by increased vices

Optimal change capability domains:

- Interpersonal: Authentic, creative connection to self and others
- Physical: Energy and endurance-focused
- Emotional: Self-aware and optimally responsive
- Intellectual: Focused, mental flexibility and systems thinking
- Social: Belonging and contributing
- Occupational: Feels psychologically safe, purpose-driven and appreciated
- Spiritual: Fulfilled, demonstrates compassion and peace

Let's explore each level of the Lead the Change Model in more detail.

THE CHANGE SURVIVOR (LEVEL I)

At Level 1, you are missing in action and trying to be unseen by all. You are underneath the ashes of change overload and burnout. It is likely that you are operating from a consciously unaware state. Your mind, body and spirit have surpassed cognitive overload, exhaustion and perhaps even hopelessness. You have either exited your industry or, at the very least, are ruminating about it.

As a Change Survivor, you relate to the following statements:

- I am psychologically and physically battle-scarred by past and present change efforts.
- I am emotionally checking out and functioning in apathetic 'get shit done' mode.
- I am succumbing to the silent pull of change overload and burnout.

THE CHANGE MINIMISER (LEVEL 2)

By Level 2, you've realised your own ineptness and you have acknowledged this inwardly. Necessity for something or anything to change in your life builds to a sufficient state where you consciously decide to allow curiosity to creep in, even if only in small increments. You are operating in 'need-to-know' mode. However, you have begun to narrowly open the door with regard to change awareness.

As a Change Minimiser, you relate to the following statements:

- I am relying on armouring up and masking to get through each day.
- I am recognising that avoidance, resistance and blame may no longer be serving me.
- I am unsure of available support, resources and possibilities.

THE CHANGE NAVIGATOR (LEVEL 3)

By Level 3, you have shifted out of inaction. There is evidence to show that you are actively shifting internal mindsets and external behaviours. As your curiosity builds, so does your patience with those around you.

As a Change Navigator, you relate to the following statements:

- I am identifying internal antagonists and allies to overcome change.
- I am moving from judgement of self and others to acceptance.
- I am shifting from 'doing' to 'being' mindsets and behaviours.

THE CHANGE ENGAGER (LEVEL 4)

By Level 4, you have consciously awakened to the transformational possibilities that change capability presents. You are self-empowering and empowering of others. It is clear you have made strong regenerative progress.

As a Change Engager, you relate to the following statements:

- I am intention-oriented.
- I am comfortable with discomfort.
- I am stepping into my inner power by engaging with future-focused initiatives.

THE CHANGE INFLUENCER (LEVEL 5)

By Level 5, you are a recognised and respected voice who knows how to strike a chord with those around you. You have a notable stance towards change and see this as one of your strengths. By now, you are not only influencing change culture but also commercial outcomes. This new resourcefulness has strengthened your ability to connect and collaborate across the organisation. You have shifted from driving people to driving change, focusing on intention, ideation and impact. You are on the road to unleashing your potential and the potential of those around you.

As a Change Influencer, you relate to the following statements:

- I am unmoved by chaos, conflict and critics.
- I am practising mastery of change capability.
- I am a change enthusiast (just ask anyone!).

THE CHANGE OPTIMISER (LEVEL 6)

Congratulations – you've made it to Level 6! At this stage, you are leading the disruption by meeting and making your own waves of change. Your future-focused mindset precedes you, and your legacy extends beyond the organisation to external communities of influence. While others are entrenched in conservatism, co-dependency and compliance, your key pillars centre around connection, collaboration and creativity. The energy and enthusiasm that you have for creative work is magnetic. This means you're in high demand for special projects and future leadership opportunities.

As a Change Optimiser, you relate to the following statements:

- I am directional with my energy, my mindset and my change trajectory.
- I am regularly contributing, collaborating and co-creating in meaningful ways.
- I advocate for others to *Reimagine Change*.

Don't leave your choices to chance. Choose to level up to the art of what is possible within yourself. Remember, it doesn't matter where you are right now. What matters is that you shift your focus towards growth and contribution.

BE AWARE (BUT NOT AFRAID) OF IMPOSTER SYNDROME

Full disclosure: I am a big, okay, huge, *Survivor* fan. If you're not familiar with the reality TV series, here is a brief overview. Each season, contestants are grouped into 'tribes' on a tropical island to 'outwit, outlast, outplay' until one of them is granted the title of 'sole survivor'. The sole survivor becomes a legacy player and goes on to collect prize money.

Viewers watching from the comfort of their lounge rooms follow the contestants as they endure harrowing weather conditions, limited food supplies, gruelling physical challenges, social trust dilemmas and inner psychological warfare.

One of the key twists is when a contestant finds a hidden immunity idol, or a clue to help them find one. An immunity idol prevents them from being voted out at tribal council and keeps them safe in the game for another week.

An immunity idol is a physical object that represents self-efficacy. It shifts the contestant's mindset from despair to hope, from being on the bottom to surviving another week, and it can even enable the contestant to win the whole game.

In the era of exponential change, each of us secretly longs to achieve that inner knowledge and self-certainty that everything will turn out in our favour. The reality is that in change psychology, there is no such thing as a hidden immunity idol. In its place is the knowledge that survival is dependent on continuous learning, upskilling and adaptiveness.

When you find yourself stretching for growth and transformation, your mind challenges your behaviour, your thinking and your skillset. So much so that you may experience imposter syndrome. In a TEDx Talk titled 'How you can use imposter syndrome to your benefit', Atlassian co-founder Mike Cannon-Brookes shared his own experience of imposter syndrome:

'So for me, imposter syndrome is a feeling of being well, well out of your depth, yet already entrenched in the situation. Internally, you know you're not skilled enough, experienced enough or qualified enough to justify being there, yet you are there, and you have to figure a way out, because you can't just get out. It's not a fear of failure, and it's not a fear of being unable to do it. It's more a sensation of getting away with something, a fear of being discovered, that at any time, someone is going to figure this out. And if they did figure it out, you'd honestly think, "Well, that's fair enough, actually."

'But it's important to note that it's not all bad. There's a lot of goodness, I think, in those feelings. And this isn't some sort of motivational-poster type talk, a "Begin it now." It's more of an introspection into my own experiences of imposter syndrome, and how I've tried to learn to harness them and turn them into some sort of a force for good.

'One, I realised that other people felt this as well. And two, I realised it doesn't go away with any form of success. I had assumed that successful people didn't feel like frauds, and I now know that the opposite is more likely to be true.

'But the most successful people I know don't question themselves, but they do heavily question, regularly question, their ideas and their knowledge. They know when the water is way too deep, and they're not afraid to ask for advice. They don't *see that as a bad thing. And they use that advice to hone those ideas, to improve them and to learn. And it's okay to be out of your depth sometimes. I'm frequently out of my depth. It's okay to be out of your depth. It's okay to be in a situation where you just can't push the eject button, so long as you don't freeze, so long as you harness the situation, don't be paralysed and try to turn it into some sort of a force for good. And it's important that I say "harness" here, because this isn't sort of pop-psychology BS about conquering imposter syndrome for me. It's merely about being aware of it.'*

Aside from this talk being a very open display of human vulner-ability for a CEO, Mike Cannon-Brookes highlights the power of self-awareness and introspection. Atlassian, the Australian start-up success story, took on the global tech giants and, as of 2020, became a $50 billion business. I especially like that one of Atlassian's five company values is:

'Be the change you seek: All Atlassians should have the courage and resourcefulness to spark change – to make better our products, our people, our place. Continuous improvement is a shared responsibility. Action is an independent one.'

Next time self-doubt creeps in, consider flipping the script and asking yourself whether you have the courage and resourcefulness to spark change.

CHAPTER SUMMARY

That brings us to the end of Chapter 2. By now, you should feel that the onus is on you to respond in a more accountable way than you may have in the past. Note that when you begin to respond differently, there may be some pushback, which will include both internal and external reactivity.

In Chapter 3, we'll discuss the impact of mental exhaustion on your brain. Before we dive into that, let's review the key points discussed in Chapter 2:

- Even when the circumstances aren't in your favour, challenge your thinking and your choices. Remember that it pays to be an opportunist rather than a quitter.

- Call time on the six antagonists (your handbrakes) holding you back. They are:
  > Avoiding your reality
  > Masking your emotions
  > Attaching via co-dependency
  > Shaming oneself
  > Blaming external forces
  > Isolating from connection

- Call in your three allies (your accelerators) to shift you forward. They are:
  > Self-awareness
  > Self-accountability
  > Self-mobilisation

- Commit to levelling up to one of the optimal Milestone Identities to 'lead the change'. The six Milestone Identities – in order of least optimal to most optimal – are:
  > Change Survivor (Level 1)
  > Change Minimiser (Level 2)
  > Change Navigator (Level 3)
  > Change Engager (Level 4)
  > Change Influencer (Level 5)
  > Change Optimiser (Level 6)

- Remain open-minded about imposter syndrome, which tends to creep into your mind during periods of personal development, growth and transformation.

- Remember that when you 'lead the change', you are liberated, energised, adaptive and disruptive.

CHAPTER 3

RECLAIM YOUR BRAIN

'Anxiety was born in the very same moment as mankind.
And since we will never master it, we will need to live
with it – just as we have learned to live with storms.'
— PAULO COELHO

tephen Spielberg's cult classic movie *Jaws* perpetuated fear
in the minds of cinemagoers long after the summer of 1975.
The star of the movie is none other than a great white shark
threatening to end peak tourism season at a coastal town. The
local authorities are keen to cover it up to minimise any negative
impact on local tourism.

In the opening scene, viewers witness a young woman taking a
twilight swim, before being violently taken by a shark. The first
of what becomes a string of attacks is covered up by declaring
the woman died in a boating accident. Once the deaths begin to
multiply, the external experts are called in, symbolising a shift in
the severity of the issue at hand. Jaws is getting out of hand. Now,
the experts not only have to venture into the water, the shark's
natural habitat, but also venture inside the mind of the shark if
they are to stand any chance of killing it.

By the end of the movie, three of the men are out in the deep ocean on their fishing boat. And what becomes evident is that they are no match for Jaws. During the final scenes (spoiler!), the last fisherman standing resorts to wedging an oxygen tank in the shark's mouth. Clinging to the crow's nest of the sinking boat, he takes one final shot and connects with the tank. Boom! The shark explodes and the fisherman lives to tell the tale. The movie went on to receive a string of accolades while viewers went on to develop a deep fear of the ocean for years to follow.

There are many lessons that can be explored through the lens of an infamous great white shark. Similar to chronic stress and burnout, everyone assumes that such a significant event 'could never happen to me'. But the only difference between a shark attack and burnout is that one takes place in the ocean, and the other in the concrete jungle.

In the movie, the character named Quint smashes the boat's radio so that the coast guard cannot be contacted. This is similar to how a person experiencing overwhelm and burnout may act. They are often too proud to reach out for help, instead preferring to go it alone and work in solitude to resolve the issue at hand. This is a risky route to take. If the battle with burnout escalates, this can lead to significant mental health issues. So, how do you address burnout before it's too late? The answer lies within.

The next chapter, 'Regenerate your body', will discuss ways to address your *physical* exhaustion. In this chapter, we'll discuss ways to address your *mental* exhaustion – and how you can 'reclaim' your brain.

UNDERSTANDING THE THREE Os

The introduction of this book is titled 'Overloaded, overwhelmed and over it'. I introduced you to Jack, who was experiencing all three of these things – and suffering immensely as a result.

To help you better understand why the 'three Os' are so damaging, here's a quick overview of the impact they can have on your mental state:

Overloaded: What you are experiencing is no longer acute stress. It is a mental state called *brain-fry or cognitive overload*. Your brain, which you rely on heavily for thinking and decision making, has reached its bandwidth and is short-circuiting.

Overwhelmed: What you are experiencing is a strong emotional response to your current experience. In relation to change fatigue, what you will notice is that the cognitive overload will be accompanied by further frustration and stress. In turn, this will further reduce your executive brain functioning. It's a classic lose/lose situation.

Over it: What you are experiencing is highly subjective, so you are best positioned to articulate what 'over it' means to you. For example, one person may shut up their laptop and call it a night, while another may hand in their resignation, never to return.

When your brain is burned out and fried, the last thing you want is a lecture about stress management. What you need to know is *how* the brain responds in a constant state of overwhelm and *how* you can brace for further impact. That's the focus of the next section.

LIFE'S A BEACH

It can be hard to come to terms with the fact that your old coping mechanisms have let you down. As a result, your brain is on constant high alert and you can't turn off the stress response.

Let's start by simplifying the feelings of stress, overwhelm and homeostasis using the following three metaphors:

1. The surf conditions (your experience of stress)
2. The shark alarm (your experience of overwhelm)
3. The surf lifesaver (your experience of homeostasis)

I. THE SURF CONDITIONS

You've arrived at the beach and you head down towards the red and yellow flags where the lifeguards recommend you swim. You hear a surf report on the crackly speakers with a word of warning about today's surf conditions. Armed with this information, low-level anxiety surfaces as you stand on the shoreline, trying to make sense of the surf report you just heard. Buoyed by courage, you enter the water and begin to navigate the waves. After some time, fatigue begins to set in. This feeling of tiredness is from repeatedly diving under the waves, wishing for more recovery time before the next set rolls in.

Conditions have changed and uncertainty now splashes around you. Boom! You've been dumped and it's rattled you to your core. You are in shock as you have always regarded yourself as a confident swimmer (up until now, that is). The waves around you are like a washing machine. Boom! You get dumped again and survival mode kicks in. If you have experienced being dumped by a wave, you know how terrifying it can feel. Your whole world narrows in and it is beyond distressing.

Then comes the turning point. Thrashing and panic is replaced by stillness. Your body is limp, exactly as it is intended. This is the body's last attempt to redirect your remaining energy into keeping your neck and head in the optimal position for your mouth and airways to take in air. This is why drowning is so silent.

This metaphor demonstrates that, regardless of experience and expertise, conditions can change in an instant and this can catch you by surprise. Even the best leaders with the best intentions may find that old coping mechanisms are no longer serving them. When stress catches you off guard, it affects you in four key ways:

- **Emotionally:** You feel negative emotions such as anxiety, fear, anger or guilt. Your energy levels deplete.
- **Physiologically:** The stress hormone, cortisol, charges through your body. Your body's anti-anxiety or anti-depression chemical, serotonin, depletes to sub-optimal levels.
- **Physically:** Your heart rate increases. Your general breathing becomes more rapid, with panic attacks and insomnia becoming your new norm.
- **Psychologically:** Rational habits and responsiveness are replaced by either conflict avoidance or bursts of irrational reactivity that tend to be overly emotional.

2. THE SHARK ALARM

To understand what is going on in your brain during overwhelm, imagine you are back at the beach. But this time, the shark alarm is sounding. Chaos erupts and the feeling of overwhelm wraps around you like a giant beach towel. Only it's not the lifeguards sounding the shark alarm – it's the amygdala in your brain. The amygdala is in charge of the emotional brain and is designed to keep you safe.

When the shark alarm sounds, this activates your survival instinct, known as the fight-or-flight response. During this time, your prefrontal cortex, the thinking or executive brain, is programmed to take cover and await instructions. At the lower end of the spectrum, stress and anxiety simply trigger the shark alarm. However, at the higher end, post-traumatic stress disorder (PTSD) will keep the shark alarm sounding off.

In a state of overwhelm, it is only when the emotional brain has sufficiently scanned the environment for safety cues – and taken any immediate action required to avoid or minimise the threat – that it calls upon the executive brain to re-enter the scene and neutralise the situation. This relies on what's called homeostasis. Homeostasis is the human body's ability to maintain and regulate your heart rate, temperature, glucose and metabolism via the autonomic nervous system (ANS). In his book *The Neuroscience of Mindfulness*, neuroscientist Stan Rodski says you know when homeostasis is out of balance by four tell-tale signs:

- **Intuition:** You endlessly question yourself and your decisions.
- **Intelligence:** You are unable to make a decision without evidence.
- **Emotions:** You fly off the handle, either overexcited or sullen and depressed.
- **Instinct:** You act without thinking in a very impulsive, automatic way.

The key insight from this is that when the emotional brain is in charge, the executive brain is disabled temporarily. That may not sound like a big deal, but in the corporate arena it is. You see, critical thinking is housed in the thinking brain, so overwhelm is not going to support your business or career efforts to lead change and disruption in this state.

3. THE SURF LIFESAVER

Back to homeostasis. For the human body to function at an optimal level, there are biological and neurological factors that facilitate homeostasis (internal equilibrium). Think of homeostasis like your inner surf lifesaver. It has dual responsibilities to protect lives both on the sand and in the surf. A surf lifesaver must oscillate between sand and surf capabilities. In other words, your surf lifesaver is responsible for effectively alternating between your fight-or-flight response and your rest-and-digest response.

Your surf lifesaver is not alone. Backing him or her up is the autonomic nervous system that has two types of surfboards to combat different surf conditions – a short board and a long board. Think of the *short board* as the *sympathetic nervous system* (*SNS*), which facilitates your fight-or-flight response and prepares you to react at high speeds to stressors. Remember that these stressors are not always negative. It is these same stressors that act as positive motivation to achieve your goals.

Meanwhile, the *long board* is the *parasympathetic nervous system* (*PNS*), which facilitates homeostasis through rest-and-digest activities. After the flight-or-flight response has been activated and the body signals that you are no longer in immediate danger, the rest-and-digest response activates to counter the effects and return your body to homeostasis. Your brain and body take great comfort in regularity and familiarity. This is because they do not trigger your fight-or-flight response and that makes you feel safe and secure. As a result, this helps your body to deeply relax or, as the surfers would say, 'hang 10'.

So, how does this play out in the real world? If you start the day by rushing to get yourself and your family out the door before walking into a day of meetings and need-now demands, you are living with an over-activated fight-or-flight response. This fight-or-flight response served us well when we were cavemen who lived in tribes and needed to be wary of life-threatening situations, like predators and invasions. However, in the modern, concrete jungle, there is a downside to over-activation of the fight-or-flight response.

SAME STORM, DIFFERENT BOAT

Over the past two decades, advances in behavioural sciences have resulted in an explosion of new theories and models. Below are six models that provide the scientific context for brain behaviour:

1. Hierarchy of needs (humanistic psychology)
2. Triune brain (evolutionary psychology)
3. PERMA model (positive psychology)
4. SCARF model (neuroleadership)
5. Mindset and neuroplasticity (psychology and neuroscience)
6. System 1 and System 2 (behavioural economics)

I. HIERARCHY OF NEEDS

In 1943, humanistic psychologist Abraham Maslow presented the hierarchy of needs. The well-known triangle initially covered five 'basic human needs'. However, this was later updated in 1970 to include a further three elements.

Needs refer to intrinsic motivators. In more recent years, neuroscience has validated a selection of Maslow's findings. Here are the original five elements of the hierarchy of needs, plus three more recent additions:

The original five...

- **Physiological needs:** Fundamentals like air, water, food, shelter and sleep.
- **Safety needs:** A sense of personal security and employment.
- **Belonging needs:** Love, compassion, connection and friendship.
- **Esteem needs:** Respect, recognition, status and fairness.
- **Self-actualisation needs:** The desire to become the most that one can become.

And three more recent additions...

- **Cognitive needs:** Knowledge, exploration and a need for meaning.
- **Aesthetical needs:** An appreciation and search for beauty and form in nature.
- **Transcendence needs:** Motivated beyond one's self via service to others, faith and sexuality.

Right now, organisations are racing to capitalise on transcendence needs by working up mission statements or purpose-driven models in service of others. However, without self-actualisation being supported in the first instance, service to others won't be sustainable.

Key insights

There are two key points to remember here. The first is in relation to safety. People often forget that safety encapsulates physical, emotional *and* psychological safety needs being met. The second key point is that you are multi-motivated. Once basic needs are met (physiological and safety needs), additional needs are sought out at any one time.

2. TRIUNE BRAIN

In the 1960s, neuroscientist Paul D. MacLean presented an evolutionary psychology model known as the triune brain. While it is no longer viewed as the dominating model and is no longer espoused, it remains an efficient way to understand the core brain structures and their relativity to stress.

Professor Terrence Deacon from the University of California, Berkeley, busted the myth in a *Yale Medicine Magazine* article, which concluded that the structures of the brain did not develop as the triune 'hats on top of hats view'. However, Deacon also stated, 'A lot of our contemporary advances ride on top of [MacLean's] work.' The three core elements of the triune brain are:

Primal brain (brain stem and cerebellum)

This is the oldest, most primitive brain, which is responsible for survival and fear modes. It has a binary view of the world, where the subconscious mind rapidly assesses situations as 'safe or unsafe'.

Survival responses (fight or flight, freeze and feign) are derived from body sensations and impulses.

Emotional brain (limbic system)
The limbic system and the evolution of emotions is unique to mammals. This area of the brain is responsible for motivation and memory formation. Research in this area focuses on the amygdala (your internal alarm), hippocampus and hypothalamus regions of the brain.

Executive brain (prefrontal cortex)
The prefrontal cortex, part of the neo-cortex, contributes to your more evolved conscious ability for logic, higher thinking, decision making, imagining and creating. It is also responsible for your memory storage of high repetition activities such as communicating, writing, reciting and riding a bike, to name a few.

The prefrontal cortex can be hijacked by the amygdala from the emotional brain. Think of it like an on-off switch. When the amygdala sounds the alarm to keep you safe, the prefrontal cortex shuts off so that all energy can be redirected.

Key insights
There are two key points to remember here. The first is that emotions and safety override logic. Where change is concerned, when emotional needs are not prioritised, conscious support – and the ability to think clearly and contribute creatively – is null and void. The second key point is that dis-ease becomes disease. Initial anxiety triggers an upset stomach and irregular digestion during periods of stress and overwhelm. Major downsides of over-activation include cardiovascular diseases, high blood pressure and low immunity, to name a few.

3. PERMA MODEL

Identified in 1998, Martin Seligman's PERMA model is one of many models that advocate for a life of subjective happiness and wellbeing. In psychology circles, positive psychology is viewed as a breakaway from the traditional views of focusing on a patient's problems. Instead, it focuses on the building blocks for a good life. These include strengths and virtues to overcome learned helplessness, and attitudes of learned optimism to fulfil authentic happiness.

In a world where mental illness is ever-increasing, the PERMA model provides a much-needed alternative mental health model to promote flourishing and optimal mental health. The five core elements of the PERMA model are:

- **Positive emotions:** Feeling good through self-generated optimism and enjoyment.
- **Engagement:** Being challenged and finding fulfilment through feel-good activities and hobbies.
- **Relationships:** Authentic connections and emotional bonds that provide you with support.
- **Meaning:** Having a purposeful existence through meaningful connections in your life.
- **Accomplishment:** A sense of achievement and pride from setting and reaching your realistic goals.

Key insights

There are two key points to remember here. The first is that the five elements of PERMA can be viewed as the ingredients of resilience. This means that your ability to adapt from adversity is within your own hands. All of the above is already accessible to you. The second point is to focus on and fire up your mental wellbeing every day rather than on an ad-hoc basis or reactively when in need. If you don't prioritise your emotional wellness, no one else will.

4. SCARF MODEL

The neuroleadership SCARF model, developed by David Rock, is a useful model with which to understand difficult or challenging brain behaviours in response to social threats. The SCARF model first appeared on the leadership agenda after David Rock's 2008 research paper 'SCARF: A Brain-Based Model for Collaborating With and Influencing Others'.

At its core is the premise that the brain keeps us safe by minimising threats (away moves) and maximising rewards (towards moves). This is applicable to yourself and others impacted by change, as it acknowledges the initial caution or resistance (away moves) associated with change. Consider how you might zoom out on threats and zoom in on rewards to optimise future change. The five core elements of the SCARF model are:

- **Status:** Your importance and respect in relation to others.
- **Certainty:** Your ability to predict the future.
- **Autonomy:** Your perception of control over events.
- **Relatedness:** Your feeling of safety and security in relation to others.
- **Fairness:** Your perception of how fair and transparent the expectations are.

Key insights

There are two key points to remember here. The first is that safety and security is the brain's primary need. Only when this ever-present survival need has been sufficiently met will the brain willingly shift towards growth activities. This may help explain why so many people will tell you that they feel 'stuck' and are unable to make progress, even though they are trying. The second key point is that social interaction trumps money rewards. Dopamine has been found to be the key neurotransmitter that rewards the brain. This is linked to higher quality social interaction at work and not salary or bonuses. Consider how the quality and quantity of your social interactions at work could be further optimised.

5. MINDSET AND NEUROPLASTICITY

'Growth mindset' is a term coined by Stanford University psychologist Dr. Carol Dweck. In her 2006 book *Mindset: The New Psychology of Success*, Dweck shares the findings of decades of research into children's behaviour and outcomes. She states, '*Talent isn't passed down in the genes; it's passed down in the mindset.*' Growth stems from a mindset of self-belief and effort. The *challenge of the challenge*, as opposed to the end goal attainment, is what will make you resilient and mentally strong. A fixed mindset stands in contrast to a growth mindset, but neuroplasticity means you can move from the former to the latter.

Fixed mindset
Intelligence is static. This limiting belief restricts curiosity, exploration and growth. A key downside is giving up too soon on your ability to overcome challenges.

Growth mindset
Intelligence can be developed. This limitless belief, accompanied by perseverance, results in the flourishing of outstanding accomplishment.

Neuroplasticity

Thanks to the known plasticity in your brain, research suggests you have the ability to rewire your malleable brain until you're in your eighties. How is this possible?

- *Neurogenesis* is your brain's ability to continuously regenerate new neurons.
- *Synaptic wiring* then results from continuous learning and repetition. This creates and strengthens the brain's neural connections and pathways. In essence, that is what is meant by the expression 'neurons that fire together wire together.' Pro tip: A great metaphor for this is to imagine you are skiing down fresh powder and, throughout the day, go back and repeat the run until it becomes engrained and habitual.
- *Synaptic pruning* is your brain's ability to remove or eliminate weakened synapses to create space for regeneration. This increases the brain's network efficiency by obeying the law 'use it or lose it'. This is also why habit forming takes approximately two months to override past behaviours.
- *Self-directed neuroplasticity* is the known consciousness of deliberately training your mind, which, in turn, rewires or 'sculpts' your brain. Dr. Rick Hanson, psychologist and expert in self-directed neuroplasticity, extends that it '*means doing it (using the mind) with clarity, skilfulness and intention. The key is a controlled use of attention.*'

Key insights

There are two key points to remember here. The first is to put the effort in and see what happens. Now that you know that intelligence can be developed and guided by your growth mindset, there is nothing stopping you from becoming unstoppable.

Prioritise learning and deep work to accelerate your personal growth. The second point is: Garbage in, garbage out. Be aware that everything you repeatedly consume, experience and interact with shapes your brain, thinking and behaviours. Choose to fuel your life with energising, expansive content rather than de-energising, contractive content.

6. SYSTEM 1 AND SYSTEM 2

In the 2011 book *Thinking, Fast and Slow*, Nobel Prize winner and godfather of behavioural economics, Daniel Kahneman, presented System 1 and System 2 thinking. Kahneman's work explores how humans manage 35,000 decisions each day, both at the simple and more complex relationship level. One of Kahneman's key findings is that all of us suffer from cognitive bias (mistaken reasoning). We'll discuss this in more detail in a future chapter. For now, here is a highly simplified explanation of what influences your thinking and decision making:

System 1

System 1 thinking, also known as fast thinking or cognitive ease, is defined as intuitive and instinctive. This influences ninety-five per cent of your decision making and is effortless, unconscious and automatic. An example here would be someone with a fear of spiders; their thoughts about the spider are instant.

System 2

System 2 thinking, also known as slow thinking or cognitive strain, is defined as more rational thinking. This influences five per cent of your decision making and takes effort, focus and deliberation. An example here would be someone consciously parallel parking their car; they need to plan the manoeuvre in their mind and focus on completing it.

Key insights

There are two key points to remember here. The first key point is that feelings trump facts. Intuition or your ability to 'just know' is the dominant (emotional) response of System 1. Often, you don't realise you are using this system to make decisions. The second key point is: What you see is all there is (WYSIATI). The impulsive nature of System 1 (fast thinking) means that your brain is prone to making errors and wrong judgements. The reason for this, as explained by Kahneman, is that WYSIATI causes you to *focus on existing evidence and ignore absent evidence.*

So, make it one of your new strengths to consciously pay attention to what is missing. For example, in business, this is referred to as the 'unspoken question'. This sounds like: 'What's keeping you up at night?' 'What haven't I shared that could make the difference?' and 'What need of yours are we not meeting at this critical point in time?'

Consider spending some time deep-diving into these models at a later date. This will help to strengthen their relevance and enable you to recall them in your mind (thanks to neuroplasticity!).

CALM THE WATERS

While metaphors, models and theories build awareness and understanding, you will also need some tangible advice and easily accessible resources to aid your overwhelmed brain. Here is a selection of immediately implementable brain practices for you to start shifting forward.

In *Rewire Your Anxious Brain: How to Use the Neuroscience of Fear to End Anxiety, Panic and Worry*, neuroscientists Catherine Pittman and Elizabeth Karle state, '*The amygdala acts as a primal response, and oftentimes, when this part of the brain processes fear, you may not even understand why you are afraid. By comparison the cortex is the centre of worry – that is, obsessing, ruminating, and dwelling on things that may or may not happen.*' Distinctions like this matter, because in order to deal with stress you need to have a clear understanding as to which neurological pathway is being interrupted.

If you are experiencing *amygdala-based anxiety from the emotional brain*, this will be automatically felt in the body and not in your thoughts. Examples of this may be the jolt of adrenaline you feel as your chest tightens or you feel butterflies in your stomach, along with quickened breathing.

Alternatively, if you are experiencing *cortex-based anxiety from the executive brain*, this is where you begin to anticipate that something bad may happen in the future. As a result, your inner dialogue begins to run through possible consequences as a psychological safety check. Here, you tend to default to catastrophising and worst-case-scenario exploring. In the workplace, an example of this is feeling stressed or anxious following a restructuring announcement. While the announcement didn't state whether anyone would be made redundant, your mind is already running through what-if scenarios.

Cortex-based anxiety coping strategies include cognitive-based therapies (CBT) where you assess the process, specifically the triggers, leading into stress and work through those. Often, mindfulness meditation is then used to bring you back to the present moment rather than being locked in past or future thinking.

The most common *amygdala-based anxiety coping strategy* is to increase your daily exercise. Going for a run, taking yoga classes and sitting through meditation are all beneficial. However, for most busy executives, their typical workday doesn't allow for this. Even if it did, none of these activities truly soothe a busy executive's brain because their overactive minds are thinking the entire time. Pro tip: Take the stairs at work more often and enjoy the challenge while you are at it. This will help to regulate the surge of adrenaline pumping through your body during office hours! Please note this is significantly less enjoyable when wearing stilettos and carrying a laptop.

The next tier down is breathing exercises, designed to slow your heart rate down. In his book *The Oxygen Advantage*, Patrick McKeown, a global expert on optimal breathing, shares that if you take breathing for granted, you aren't alone. Most people are guilty of 'chronically over breathing', creating a negative feedback loop beyond just a quantity over quality issue.

Here's how to practise optimal nose breathing: Stop shallow mouth breathing and reengage the use of your nose. As you breathe lightly into your nose, focus on the air going all the way down into your diaphragm, which should be expanding out. This allows you to 'breathe less and breathe right'. The real benefit here is that nose breathing activates calm responses, whereas mouth breathing activates fight-or-flight (more panicked or impulsive) responses. This tiny tweak can be a game changer.

You should also pay attention to your heart. According to the HeartMath Institute, which has conducted over twenty-five years of scientific research into the interactions between the heart and the brain, and the impact on emotions and the body, heart coherence is essential to stress management.

Heart breathing, coupled with appreciation and gratitude, can diffuse frustration and better regulate your nervous system. This sees your body transition into a state of ease and inner harmony. HeartMath states, *'Psychologically, coherence is experienced as a calm, balanced, yet energised and responsive state that is conducive to everyday functioning and interaction, including the performance of tasks requiring mental acuity, focus, problem-solving, and decision-making, as well as physical activity and coordination.'*

Heart breathing is quick and easy to learn, so why not try it out now for the next few minutes? Here's how you do it: Focus your attention on the area of the heart. You might like to place a hand over your heart area. Imagine your breath is flowing in and out of your heart or chest area. Try breathing a little slower and deeper than usual. Inhale for five seconds, exhale for five seconds (or whatever rhythm is comfortable).

Make a sincere attempt to experience a peaceful feeling, such as appreciation or care for someone or something in your life. Try to focus on the feeling you have for someone you love, a pet, a special place or an accomplishment, or focus on a feeling of calm or ease.

In the book *You Are Not Your Brain*, Jeffrey Schwartz (neuroplasticity researcher at University of California, Los Angeles) and Rebecca Gladding (neuroleadership specialist) argue that your biology is not your destiny and that you are not fated by your genes. For some of you, this will not be new information, while, for others, it may be. The disparity occurs because most of us are never upskilled in brain behaviour, either at school (where the focus is rote learning) or at work (where the focus is expertise enhancement).

When your work involves managing and leading others, it is important to better understand the role of the brain and the mind at work. Schwartz and Gladding share that the *brain's role* is to be a neuroplasticity machine, while the *mind's role* is to either accept or reject the messages that come from the brain. In particular, you need to pay attention to cognitive distortion or 'deceptive brain messages'.

These are false thoughts and messages that come into your mind and impact your ability to optimally perform. Here's what happens: Your brain pays close attention to anything that puts you into dis-ease or upsets your sense of safety and security. It emotionally records this as important for future recall. Your brain then relies on past experiences to recall whether a person, place or situation was a positive or negative experience. If it registers as a past negative experience or, more importantly, has similar constructs to a past negative experience, it will warn you to be cautious, on guard or avoidant.

Much like the only way to regain your sense of self around a narcissist is to starve them of your attention, Schwartz and Gladding say: '*The key to making life changes that you want – to make your brain work for you – is to consciously choose to "starve" these circuits of focused attention, thereby decreasing their influence and strength.'*

Swartz and Gladding recommend four ways to override the system:

- **Relabel:** Identify intrusive thoughts and uncomfortable urges that enter your mind from your brain. Call them what they are.
- **Reframe:** Acknowledge that these are primal brain messages. You might say something like, 'That's not me – that is my brain up to its old tricks again!'
- **Refocus:** Direct all of your attention towards more wholesome and fulfilling activities. Switch from overthinking to keeping busy by taking positive action steps.
- **Revalue:** Dismiss negative thoughts and urges that linger; know that they are simply cognitive distortions. Tell yourself what you need in a loving, caring way.

Before we move on, here are four key insights to remember:

- **Befriend your brain:** Trust and respect impact social bonding and influence. Respect your brain, and learn more about how and why it functions in often irrational ways.
- **Strengthen the brain-mind relationship:** Your brain will always try to be the dominant player. However, conscious awareness allows your mind to have the upper hand.
- **Beware of cognitive distortion:** Your brain's delivery of thoughts, urges and desires can be deceptive. This influences your thinking, feeling and behavioural experiences.
- **Cultivate a mindful mind:** Simply by focusing your awareness on pausing and being present, you will now be positioned to guide your mind to higher quality answers.

LEARNING TO LET GO

Susan David, author of *Emotional Agility*, states, 'Discomfort is the price of admission to a meaningful life.' What she means by this is that it is important to come to terms with your most difficult emotions in order to be happy and reach fulfilment.

As you continue to navigate chaos and calm, I will leave you with a poem about entering fear. When you are anxious, it means you are overinvested in the future. Consider what possibilities may unfold from less attachment to the immediate change outcome. It is not easy to swim upstream in fear. Sometimes, the answer lies in letting go of your stronghold or investment in the future. The topic of fear will be explored in more detail in the next chapter. For now, I leave you with this poem.

'FEAR' BY KAHLIL GIBRAN

It is said that before entering the sea
a river trembles with fear.

She looks back at the path she has travelled,
from the peaks of the mountains,
the long winding road crossing forests and villages.

And in front of her,
she sees an ocean so vast,
that to enter
there seems nothing more than to disappear forever.

But there is no other way.
The river cannot go back.

Nobody can go back.
To go back is impossible in existence.

The river needs to take the risk
of entering the ocean
because only then will fear disappear,
because that's where the river will know
it's not about disappearing into the ocean,
but of becoming the ocean.

CHAPTER SUMMARY

That brings us to the end of Chapter 3. By now, you should have a newfound respect for your mighty brain. However, with knowledge comes great power. Now, you can draw on that knowledge to better manage your stress and regulate your emotions.

In the transition from Part 1 to Part 2, we'll discuss the importance of shifting from KNOW to GROW. Before we dive into that, let's review the key points discussed in Chapter 3:

- Metaphors help to highlight the distinction between feelings of stress, overwhelm and homeostasis. In the context of a day at the beach, these feelings can be likened to:
  - > The surf conditions (your experience of stress)
  - > The shark alarm (your experience of overwhelm)
  - > The surf lifesaver (your experience of homeostasis)

- Research advances in the field of behavioural sciences have resulted in an explosion of new theories and models. The six explored in this chapter were:
  - > Hierarchy of needs (humanistic psychology)
  - > Triune brain (evolutionary psychology)
  - > PERMA model (positive psychology)
  - > SCARF model (neuroleadership)
  - > Mindset and neuroplasticity (psychology and neuroscience)
  - > System 1 and System 2 (behavioural economics)

- Immediate resources are at your disposal when you are seeking calmness. These include:

  > Coping strategies for amygdala and cortex-based anxiety
  > Nose and heart breathing practices
  > Relabel/Reframe/Refocus/Revalue practice

FROM PART 1 TO PART 2

'You don't determine your opportunities;
you determine your readiness.'

– MARK MILLER

n Part 1: KNOW, we tapped into the importance of realising the severity of the issues at hand and being accountable for responding to them. Key resources gathered so far include self-affirmation, self-mobilisation and self-awareness.

In Part 2: GROW, we will explore the 'how' component. Beyond self-affirmation, self-mobilisation and self-awareness is self-realisation. Self-realisation is achievable through regenerating, recoding and reimagining your change identity. As you learned in the last chapter, without self-mobilisation, you risk going backwards.

So, if you know that going back to the depths of change fatigue and burnout is not an option, then let's take a look at what's on the horizon.

Here are some questions to keep in mind as you move through each chapter in Part 2:

REGENERATE your body: What is the impact of unattended

trauma and fear on the body? Chapter 4 gives you permission to explore care, compassion and human connection.

RECODE your mind: What mindset strategies will set you up for success? Chapter 5 asks you to deep-dive into your subconscious mind.

REIMAGINE your creativity: How might igniting your imagination and creativity benefit your journey? Chapter 6 will show you how to prime for greater change contribution.

Let's get into it!

PART 2

GROW

CHAPTER 4

REGENERATE YOUR BODY

'Nothing will work unless you do.'

– Maya Angelou

B etween 1977 and 2019, this mega franchise produced nine films and countless media extensions totalling an estimated US$70 billion. If you've guessed *Star Wars*, you are right! To switch things up, let's now go behind the camera and tap into the inspiration for this epic film franchise.

Did you know that George Lucas was actually a super fan of Joseph Campbell's writings and used them as a reference for the original *Star Wars* trilogy? In 1949, Joseph Campbell authored *The Hero with a Thousand Faces*. Campbell explores the idea of heroism and personal transformation through 'the hero's journey' and 'archetype' concepts.

In essence, Campbell argues that in order to become the hero, you must sustain a journey. Therefore, heroism cannot be achieved from a single act of bravery. Fundamental to the hero's journey is removing barriers to change, and building resources and inner strengths to draw on when faced with future adversity. Sound familiar? Campbell outlines twelve stages in the hero's journey, but these can be distilled into three key stages:

- **Stage 1 – the departure:** The protagonist, not yet the hero, is responding to the 'call of duty' by leaving the safety of the status quo and being inspired by a 'mentor' on the way to the new world. In your case, you are reading this book and seeking some guidance to overcome overwhelm, change fatigue and burnout. You can either refuse the 'call of duty' or respond to it in a proactive manner.

- **Stage 2 – the initiation:** Next, the protagonist has to find their own way through unfamiliar territory. This requires them to overcome a succession of temptations, trials and tests, ultimately transforming them into the 'hero'. In your case, only when you stretch and challenge yourself will you achieve a new level of knowledge, perspective and wisdom. Regardless of the sub-challenges that may present themselves, the key is to keep your eye focused on the overall journey.

- **Stage 3 – the return:** Next, the hero takes their newfound wisdom and knowledge back to the 'ordinary' world, in turn, encouraging others to evolve and begin their own journey. In your case, by the time you have completed this book, my hope is that you will be confident integrating the learnings into your everyday life. Others will recognise and admire your refreshed approach to change. This may then prompt a greater shared understanding of the *Reimagine Change* framework among your team and organisation.

The hero's journey metaphor is useful in that, while it may sound egotistical to focus on your personal change capability in the first instance, it is a future of work imperative. If you truly want to be *for people* – to serve them, to inspire them and to leave a legacy for them – then you need to do the inner work on yourself first.

Remember that life is long and it pays to prepare for the journey ahead. You are not designed to be a corporate athlete; you are a human being. And humans are wonderfully complex, fragile and resilient. Despite how far you may have spiralled down, there's always an opportunity to regenerate and forge on. That is the focus of this chapter.

THE CAVE YOU FEAR

There are many ways to approach regeneration. My immediate focus is to address the correlation between organisational-change-induced burnout and the symptoms of post-traumatic stress disorder (PTSD). To do so, we are going to explore research insights regarding emotional safety and trauma. If for any reason this content causes you to feel triggered or wounded, please take as much time as you require to regroup before continuing on.

Awareness and appreciation of trauma, and what it entails, can result in 'aha' moments for yourself and those in your care. These learnings can then be applied to build mental strength and emotional resilience within yourself. They're also likely to crack any hard exterior you may have developed, allowing real empathy to be extended to others who may have endured past trauma or corporate suffering.

Trauma is the emotional response to and outcome of a traumatic event. Examples of traumatic events include death, divorce, birth, car accidents, rape, natural disasters, parental abandonment and abuse (physical or emotional). Examples of emotional trauma in the workplace include events where you may have felt unaware, unprepared or powerless to prevent the event. This includes organisational stressors such as retrenchment, rapid business transformation and organisational change that impact your work identity, your job and how you are used to delivering your work to the best of your ability. Trauma lives on inside our mind and body, often hidden or just below the surface like a cave within a mountain.

When someone is experiencing trauma, the body's natural response activates. Beyond the more common fight-or-flight response is the freeze response. The term 'freeze' is evident when you 'become a dear in headlights', 'stop dead in your tracks' or 'collapse in the moment'. Here, your subconscious mind (the storehouse of beliefs) is in extreme protection mode because your ability to fight or take flight is no longer a choice. In the animal kingdom, this is where animals pretend they are dead to encourage the predator to move on more quickly.

The freeze response activates in response to extreme fear and trauma. In the absence of hope that you can out flee or fight your way out of your scenario, the freeze response activates. This is your body's way of keeping you safe. Your body becomes immobilised, like cement. You are frozen on the spot, filled with dread. You may not be sure you are even breathing anymore. Dissociation may take place, whereby you mentally 'check out' of the situation you find yourself in.

At the lower level of the dissociation spectrum, this may feel as though you are in a haze and disconnected from your physical body, which, in turn, diminishes your ability to concentrate. One of three elements of 'crash and burn' explored earlier, depersonalisation (feeling emotionally numb), is another example of this.

When fears are left unaddressed or repressed, they transition into anxiety. You become a 'nervous wreck'. When anxiety and tension continue to grow, this lived state is now recognised as post-traumatic stress disorder (PTSD). Another way to think of this is as a psychological wound that hinders optimal functioning.

PTSD symptoms include but are in no way limited to:

- High reactivity (perceived as being resistant)
- Hyper-vigilant behaviours (perceived as being tense)
- Mistrust of others (perceived as being stand-offish)
- Sporadic emotional outbursts (perceived as having a low EQ)
- Low spectrum dissociation and flashbacks (perceived as being zoned out)

PAUSE & REFLECT

Do any of these symptoms ring true for you? You may like to spend a few minutes journaling about whatever arises in relation to this.

YOUR BODY KEEPS SCORE

In 1994, neuroscientist Dr Stephen Porges developed the Polyvagal Theory. This ground-breaking research sent ripples around the world as a glimmer of hope for those experiencing and living with PTSD.

Polyvagal Theory offers an in-depth insight into the intense emotional and physiological symptoms of PTSD. The following content outlines the top-down or hierarchy system relative to the individual experience of safety. In other words, when your individual needs for psychological and physical safety are not met, your body sequences down through the three following reactions.

OVERWHELMED STATE (SEEKING SAFETY)

- **First reaction:** Social engagement; 'I seek connection'

Here, the social-support response initiates and you actively seek out trust, engagement and support of others. When the seeking of social support is repeatedly unavailable, you turn to vices, as outlined in previous chapters. The mind is racing; the body remains calm.

- **Second reaction:** Mobilisation; 'I'm in danger'

Here, the ventral vagal system is overridden by sympathetic system activation. Initially, the flight response initiates. However, this defaults to the fight response when you sense your options are limited. Verbal and physical reactivity peaks. The mind is racing and the body is on high alert from increases in your heart rate and hormones.

- **Third reaction:** Immobilisation; 'I can't cope, I'm shutting down, I'm scared stiff'

Here, the dorsal vagal system turns on. The collapse response initiates to shut you off from the inevitable (perceived or real) threat. The mind automatically shuts down in the form of dissociation, freezing and shock. Feeling trapped and intensely frightened, your speech centre shuts down, your heart rate drops and your body recoils.

OPTIMAL STATE (SENSING SAFETY)

- **First reaction:** Social engagement; 'I feel safe, secure, social and connected'

You sense safety from facial expression, vocalisation and listening. You are a valued tribe member. When connection is trusted, bonds deepen and vulnerabilities are shared.

- **Second reaction:** Mobilisation; 'I'm free to be me'

You engage in play states such as humour and exercise. You seek ways to positively channel your energy. This ranges from being curious to seeking more adventure.

- **Third reaction:** Resting for rejuvenation; 'I forecast the need to conserve energy'

You carve out time to rest and prepare for future social engagement. You and your body recognise this as a value investment.

PAUSE & REFLECT

- Have you experienced a time when you sought out safety and connection in the workplace?
- If such safety was unavailable, do you remember how your body handled this?
- How might your work environment (e.g. open-plan setting or perhaps hot-desking) trigger your hyper-vigilant state? Does movement behind you bother you, are you unable to filter out the noise, and does the lack of privacy keep your nervous system on edge (either consciously or subconsciously) rather than laser focused on the value of your work?
- What steps could you take to reorient towards a more 'safe and sound' community and environment?

Dr. Porges' theory also explores the term 'neuroception', as show in Figure 6. This is where your neural circuits in your nervous system are subconsciously scanning others and the environment to assess perceived safety, risk factors and trustworthiness. It is the subconscious equivalent of airport security. And yes, this occurs outside of your conscious awareness! For example, you may subconsciously ask yourself: Is this other person safe to be around? Should I engage with them? Should I trust them? Yes, this applies within your workplace, too. For every interaction, your neuroception is internally scanning.

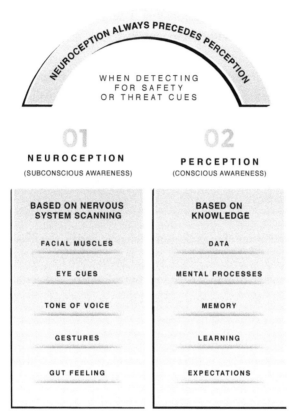

Figure 6: Neuroception always precedes perception.
Reimagine Change interpretation of neuroception and Polyvagal Theory (Porges, 2011).

Here, your body involuntarily senses three levels or autonomic states to depict safety:

- **Green light: Safe (normal, social functioning; mammalian response).** To use a traffic light metaphor, you have a green light, indicating an openness to social engagement.

- **Amber light: Danger (prepare for fight or flight; reptilian response).** In this autonomic state, you have an amber light, indicating a transition to mobility.

- **Red light: Life-threatening (activate the freeze response; reptilian response).** In this autonomic state, you have a red light, indicating immobility or a complete shutdown.

Conquering your fears is not about ignoring them or running away. It is about acknowledging them for what they are and moving through them.

The perception of organisational change versus the lived experience of it are vastly different. Experiencing peak periods of change heightens your brain's need for control, safety and certainty. To live a healthy, happy and optimal life, you need to feel safe.

Externally, this is why psychological safety is an imperative at work. Without it, a culture of calm and connection will be absent. This then restricts your ability to engage in focus, deep work, trust, collaboration and innovation. Culture aside, what are some ways you can coach yourself to safer grounder?

Internally, this means that your dominant state or baseline needs to be the safe state, with a stimulated vagus nerve. The vagus nerve is a cranial nerve that runs from the brain down to the abdomen. It is linked to all of the organs within the autonomic nervous system.

Key insights to cultivate the safe state:

- **Be aware of the window of tolerance:** This is the space between hyperarousal (fight or flight) and hypoarousal (dis-association and shutting down), where your prefrontal cortex is engaged.
- **Foster positive social connection:** Cut out, minimise and avoid de-energising or toxic individuals and groups. Remember that neutral and negative facial cues signal danger.
- **Seek out safe environments:** Record environments where your body feels unsafe. Then integrate safer locations into your week. Use flexible working arrangements if available.
- **Move your body:** Exert any residual energy in your body by doing light exercise that you recognise as positively influencing your mood. This will be different for each of you.

Breath work is one way to stimulate the vagus nerve. Remember, the vagus nerve is linked to all of the organs within the autonomic nervous system. However, the lungs are the only organ within the autonomic nervous system that you can directly influence in real time. That's why breath work is so effective.

Key insights to stimulate the vagus nerve:

- **Breath work:** Practice intentional, long, slow breathing, remembering that, ideally, the out breath needs to be twice as long as the in breath. Focus on the mantra 'safe and secure'.
- **Humming:** Choose your favourite song and hum the entire song to promote full throat vibration. Alternatives to humming are singing or gargling to stimulate your throat.
- **Diving reflex:** Splash your face with cold water, take a cold

shower or submerge your tongue in a warm drink. This will divert or pattern-interrupt your nervous system.

- **Connecting with people who care:** Seek out a friendly face in person or a soothing tone of voice over the phone to signal to your ears to reengage your social engagement system.

Dr. Peter Levine, a psychologist and author of *Waking the Tiger: Healing Trauma*, states, *'Trauma is a fact of life. It does not have to be a life sentence.'* Dr. Levine is also the creator of somatic experiencing, which is a neurophysical understanding of trauma. It is *'a clinical methodology as to why animals in the wild are not traumatised by routine threats to their lives, while humans, on the other hand, are readily overwhelmed and often subject to the traumatic symptoms of hyper-arousal, shutdown and dysregulation.'* Levine recommends a self-holding exercise to help soothe the nervous system.

Here's how you do it: Either lying down or seated in your chair, close your eyes and gently place one hand on your forehead and the other hand on your heart. Stay like this for as long as you like. During this time, focus your attention on the mind-body connection and notice when there is a 'sensing' shift. This could last for three minutes or thirty minutes. Next, move your hand from your forehand to your stomach, so one hand is across the heart and the other is on the stomach. Repeat the same process as before. Take as much time as you need to remain in this self-nurturing state.

Nervous system know-how will soon become as mainstream as yoga. Why? Because your body keeps score of the damage being done. And until you attend to it, you will remain in a constant state of hypervigilance, unable to relax, switch off or be at ease.

Recognising that your nervous system can be unintentionally triggered, retriggered and self-soothed is crucial to your regeneration.

RECOVERY + RESILIENCE = REGENERATION

You can't be future ready if you are battling, day in, day out, with the psychological warfare taking place in your head (mind) and your body (nervous system). You either have to stop at some point or be stopped. Prior to starting this journey, you may have thought that what you need is more resilience. There are two primary reasons why individuals seek out resilience:

- **Reactivity:** You are currently under siege and need a lifeline out.
- **Proactivity:** You are expecting more change and want to prepare for that.

If you're looking for a lifeline, it's important to understand that resilience is not realistic without the pre-phase of recovery. Only when the body has returned to homeostasis – its optimal oscillation between the parasympathetic and the sympathetic states – can the brain optimise and begin to heal and repair itself. Recovery will fast-track this. It is the powerful combination of recovery and resilience that allows you to regenerate. For this to happen, you need to allow time and space for mindful solitude. Before we go there, let's now spotlight one aspect of resilience that is often overlooked.

An important aspect of resilience is to regain a sense of control in your life. Locus of control is a psychological construct used to describe attitudes and behaviours. It is a bridging concept between social and behavioural psychology.

At one end of the continuum is the external locus of control. Here, you believe that the results you have in life are a by-product of external influence. More specifically, someone or something is responsible for the negative results in your life. At the other end of the continuum is the internal locus of control. Here, you believe that outcomes can be directly attributed to *your* effort, attitude and choices. The locus of control mindset is, in essence, positive self-talk that spurs you on to be courageous, curious and independent. During drastic change and adversity, this can feel challenging at the best of times. This is where mindful solitude can play a supportive role.

PRACTISING MINDFUL SOLITUDE

It's important to recognise that the environment that has produced your change fatigue is not going to be the ideal environment for you to begin alleviating your exhaustion and overwhelm. Ideally, you should take some time away from your job if you are experiencing workplace burnout. The alternative of 'just keeping going' is not going to do you any favours. In fact, it is likely to weaken your resilience. This will see environmental and human triggers – such as the meeting room where people are let go, or hostile or anxious co-workers – continuing to retrigger you and, thus, reinforcing your negative mental state.

Right now, you may be thinking of dismissing this. The concept of mindful solitude may seem too dramatic for you. It is not.

Taking a mental health day or a holiday is not going to cut it. If you're experiencing a high level of change fatigue or burnout, this will have little to no impact. To really get to the root cause and address what is going on, you are going to need some intentional mindful solitude. This entails a break from responsibility, stillness to decompress and regenerative self-care. There is no shame in slowing down. The world will wait while you take some time to regenerate. Note that this will look and feel different for everyone, based on your work, family and financial responsibilities. Ideally, you will carve out up to two weeks by yourself or with a select few people.

The litmus test for burnout is usually two weeks. In other words, if after two weeks of mindful solitude you are still emotionally struggling, then this is a telling sign. If the same negative thoughts are dominating your mind and the same uncomfortable sensations are being experienced in your body, then you are at a significant choice point where you need to share your lived reality with a loved one, a support person and eventually your place of work.

Self-discovery and intuition lie below the surface of stillness. If your life is anything like mine used to be, full of calendar commitments and eternal rushing from here to there, stillness is rarely achievable in your current work and home environment. So, creating the conditions to access these inner resources is foundational. Pro tip: Schedule your ongoing wellbeing and mindful solitude into your work diary as a priority.

Beyond mindful solitude, there are other key components of regeneration. Namely, self-care and self-compassion. Let's explore those now.

SELF-CARE

Self-care soothes your soul, grounds you in gratitude and energises your potential. It's a regenerative, ongoing process that underpins mood improvement and stress management. When self-care is absent, you are likely to begin the downward spiral into the negative emotional states discussed in Chapter 1.

Self-care is prioritised for physical energy renewal. The two pillars of self-care are:

- Sleep prioritisation
- Fear minimisation

SLEEP PRIORITISATION

In today's busy society, there is very little empathy for fatigue, exhaustion or burnout. However, to return to being happy, healthy and future ready, you need to extend care to yourself, your loved ones and your team. The secret to sustainable success is to start with yourself. Putting yourself first is not selfish, even though, at times, it may feel like it. Remember that you are playing the long game and that is going to take an inner commitment to raising your energy.

It's not always easy to articulate what is going on when you are inside your own personal storm. So, I have created the 'significant seven energy spectrum' to help you in pinpointing what you are personally experiencing most days of the week. Where you are on the spectrum is closely linked to the quality of your sleep.

PAUSE & REFLECT

As you read through the following, consider which energy level best describes your average day.

The significant seven energy spectrum

1. **Energised:** You personify zest for life. Others recognise your enthusiasm and high energy. Your vibrancy translates into more creative, collaborative and innovative work, and other external activities. You prioritise sleep, exercise, connection and mental wellbeing.

2. **Refreshed:** You have recharged your batteries beyond your neutral state. Averaging between seven and nine hours of sleep each night readies you for a successful start to your day. When consistent, this ensures you remain in a calm, collective and positive state.

3. **Neutral:** You have experienced your 'normal' night of sleep, whether that's five hours, seven hours or whatever it might be. This meets your day-to-day individual needs but it is certainly nothing to boast about. Neutral is average at best and, deep down, you know this isn't optimal.

4. **Tired:** You have had one or two bad nights' sleep, and feel cranky and drowsy as a result. Your concentration is impacted. However, unlike fatigue, a nap or early night to bed will see you bounce back to a neutral or refreshed energy level the next morning.

5. **Fatigued:** You have transitioned from a one-off into a sleep decline pattern. This includes increased reliance on vices, lying awake ruminating, and fragmented waking in the early hours. You rarely wake refreshed. Your fatigue accompanies you everywhere during the day.

6. **Exhausted:** You have begun to socially withdraw. At work, you keep to yourself and your workload, focusing on what little you feel you have control over. Emotional numbness, functional delirium and an over-activated startle reflex are present. Five hours' sleep is rare.

7. **Burned out:** Mental and physical exhaustion have peaked. There is a high probability that either a major error in judgement, physical accident or witnessed collapse has occurred as a recognisable marker that you are burned out. Shame and vulnerability see you remove yourself from public and seek refuge either independently or via professional support.

While one bad night's sleep is manageable the next day, weeks and months of sleep debt can be detrimental to your health and wellbeing. According to research conducted by the RMIT Sleep Lab at RMIT University, sleep deprivation has four major impacts:

- Cognitive performance diminishes, impacting your capacity to reason and problem solve.
- Reaction time decreases, increasing your risk of accidents.
- Mood and emotional responses skew towards irritability and negativity.
- You have a greater risk of serious health problems that are heart or glucose related.

In Japanese, the word 'karoshi' translates to 'overwork death'. This refers to being worked to death – literally – as a result of lack of sleep and food, and increased stress and heart issues. To have an optimal brain and body, first and foremost, you must acknowledge any fatigue and attend to your sleep deprivation. Wherever you feel you are positioned on the significant seven energy spectrum, remember that you are not fixed to your current position and a shift can occur – providing you make some changes. Unlearning bad habits and upgrading your sleep hygiene will help you regain some control.

The optimal sleep hygiene

There are two ways to achieve an optimal sleep hygiene – by preparing your physical environment and by preparing yourself, mentally as well as physically. Here's a breakdown:

PREPARE YOUR ENVIRONMENT

1. **Technology:** Remove all technology from your bedroom (no televisions, no laptops, no mobile phones). You need to be strict with this to get any traction.

2. **Time:** Buy a standalone clock with an alarm (if you are a clock watcher, keep it on the ground, not at eye level – watching the minutes tick at 2am isn't doing you any favours).

3. **Light and temperature:** Install blackout curtains. Cooler room temperatures between sixteen and eighteen degrees regulate natural melatonin levels and alleviate insomnia.

4. **Declutter:** When your room is simplified and tidy, this is visually self-soothing and inviting. If possible, 'declutter' your loved one while you are at it, so that you can enjoy uninterrupted sleep.

5. **Bedding:** Invest in natural, breathable fabrics like cotton, linen, wool and silk bedding to encourage your body to rejuvenate. Weighted blankets are excellent for alleviating restlessness and anxiety.

6. **Thoughts:** Place a journal and pen by your bed (if your thoughts wake you, do not ruminate – write them down and self-soothe by attending to them in the morning).

PREPARE YOUR SELF

1. **Intention:** Every morning, praise what sleep you did get, not what sleep you didn't. This will positively prime your mind for sleep. Yes, you need to start this in the morning.

2. **Movement:** Move your body every day, ideally inviting in vitamin D via sunlight exposure by exercising outdoors when the weather permits.

3. **Vices:** Avoid alcohol prior to bed (it's dehydrating and causes waking), limit caffeine intake (no caffeine at least four to six hours before bed) and see a clinical hypnotherapist to help you quit smoking today!

4. **Nutrition:** Focus on eating more whole foods and fewer processed foods, and drink at least two litres of water per day.

Magnesium and ashwagandha have been shown to improve sleep and insomnia.

5. **Consumption:** Consume news earlier in the day (ideally around midday) and be mindful of your viewing habits late in the evening (be aware not to trigger your subconscious with any fear-inducing content).

6. **Wind down:** Set a daily reminder that signals one hour prior to bed. Switch off all technology, take a bath, journal gratitude and goals, and set up whatever you need to for the morning (like laying out your workout gear and/or office attire).

If after thirty days you are not seeing any improvement in your sleeping patterns, you may have a serious sleep disorder and should, therefore, consult a medical professional.

FEAR MINIMISATION

Once you have prioritised sleep hygiene, you will be better positioned to commence a personal cognitive intervention. Think of this as a review of the inner workings of your mind.

From an evolutionary perspective, fear is designed to help you survive. To ready you to fight or take flight in dire, life-threatening situations, like being attacked by bears or violent opposing tribes. In neuro-linguistic programming (NLP), fear is explored through the lens of individual perception and illusion. This is particularly relevant in our modern world where we are no longer battling life-threatening scenarios in the same frequency, yet, our minds and bodies are still responding with the same evolutionary responses.

The following acronym is a useful aid in this context – FEAR:

False
Evidence
Appearing
Real

By unearthing common fears, change anxiety can be addressed and minimised through a variety of strategies. It is important to understand that there is not a one-size-fits-all approach. This is because fear is a highly subjective experience. However, if your desire is for successful, sustainable change, then this will only be realised once your feelings of overwhelm, fatigue and stress have been acknowledged and addressed. Here are ten common fears associated with change, and how to overcome them.

1. Fear of the unknown

Problem: Right now, you feel uncertain of what lies ahead so your brain is filling in the gaps with assumptions and worst-case scenarios. Negativity bias sees you overemphasise negative thinking patterns.

Practice: Become better informed. Actively seek out accurate, time-specific information. List out and address your top three unresolved concerns.

2. Fear of leaving your comfort zone

Problem: You feel safe and secure within the domains of your current reality. Your brain is in overdrive with questions of 'What if?' 'Why me?' and 'Why now?'

Practice: Get the concerns out of your mind and onto paper. Consider what lies behind your self-doubt. Consider whether you are receiving sufficient emotional support from others.

3. Fear of things getting worse

Problem: You are riddled with anxious thoughts and your body senses fear in the absence of real danger. You trick yourself into thinking you have limited options.

Practice: Stop fighting fire with fire. Realise that resistance is not protecting you – it may be polarising you. Drop your guard and begin to expand your perspective.

4. Fear of self-promotion

Problem: You wrongly assume that your accomplishments speak for themselves and that self-promotion is self-centred and arrogant.

Practice: Share your successes, strengths and skills. Showcase best practices. Avoid 'comparisonitis' – keep your work consistent and authentic to who you are.

5. Fear of being judged

Problem: You guard yourself from disclosing all information regarding your true self and true capabilities. Unknowingly, this depletes your energy reserves.

Practice: Unhook from the belief that you have to people please to be accepted and get ahead.

Remember that your uniqueness is your power. Don't let others dampen that.

6. Fear of success

Problem: You are either consciously or subconsciously concerned with how the change will challenge or impact your time, energy, lifestyle and general happiness.

Practice: List out the possible positive and negative consequences. Close your eyes and check in with your future self to see if the proposed options feel good or bad. Be guided by that.

7. Fear of failure

Problem: You worry that you are not going to cope in the future environment. For example, the new technology, systems, processes or team structures may be out of your league.

Practice: Address your skill shortage concerns. Practise self-kindness to minimise any underlying perfection expectations. Seek out a supportive mentor or coach to guide you.

8. Fear of missing out

Problem: You are a social being and, as such, seek stability and connection from within your tribe. Work represents one such priority tribe where you avoid humiliation at all costs.

Practice: Consider whether humiliation or exclusion is a realistic consequence. If you sense it is, seek consultation with an authority in this area. Fill your time with joy-inducing activities.

9. Fear of being found out

Problem: You are experiencing imposter syndrome. You believe you are a fraud, regardless of your experience and accomplishments. The inner critic in your head is prominent.

Practice: Begin to unveil more of the authentic you, including strengths, weaknesses, aspirations and self-limiting beliefs. If the real you is not welcomed, you are in the wrong place.

10. Fear of abandonment

Problem: You feel vulnerable and unguarded in taking the first step into the new reality. You seek psychological safety. When it is absent, you are unable to co-regulate.

Practice: Beyond upskilling, consider what you are craving socially. Be specific. For example, reversing under-management, visible role-modelling or perhaps servant leadership.

Right now, you may be thinking this is a lot of information to digest and recall. That's why the book has been designed as a reference guide to support you. Enacting best practice in the moment requires practice, patience and perseverance. In the event that brain fog is lingering, be kind to yourself and your ability to recall new learnings.

SELF-COMPASSION

Self-compassion encompasses self-love, self-kindness and self-acceptance. It is the antidote to self-judgement, self-criticism and self-loathing, all of which surface during periods of unlearning and relearning. Mistakes, errors and failures are all part of the process of being human.

Compassion is the capacity to experience, or sit with, the associated suffering and, in response, be moved to action. It is often said that empathy plus action equals compassion. Compassion is when you *see* someone in need, *care* about them and *do* something to aid them through via your actions. Self-compassion is when you *recognise* the need within yourself, *care* for yourself and *do* something to shift yourself in a more positive direction. We'll explore an example of this in a moment.

Compassion expert Dr. Kristin Neff defines self-compassion as *'being open to and moved by one's own suffering, experiencing feelings of caring and kindness toward oneself, taking an understanding, non-judgemental attitude toward one's inadequacies and failures, and recognising that one's experience is part of the common human experience.'*

In *Nonviolent Communication: A Language of Life: Life-Changing Tools for Healthy Relationships*, the late author and psychologist Dr. Marshall Rosenberg outlines a communication process that helps people exchange the information necessary to resolve conflicts and differences peacefully. This is the book that, according to former Microsoft CEO Satya Nadella, shaped and transformed Microsoft's culture 'from cutthroat to creative'. The key hinge being the conscious moment where a leader questions where another human may be coming from, and then applies empathy and compassion to round out the equation.

Dr. Rosenberg writes:

> *'An important aspect of self-compassion is to be able to empathetically hold both parts of ourselves, the self that regrets a past action and the self that took the action in the first place. The process of mourning and self-forgiveness frees us in the direction of learning and growing. In connecting moment by*

moment to our needs, we increase our creative capacity to act in harmony with them.'

A key insight to remember here is that we are all energetic equals. Power plays aside, your ability to connect with others and yourself from a standpoint of common humanity is what true connection, belonging and collaboration is all about.

Compassion requires you to connect with others, to be with them and for them. Self-compassion requires you to apply the same principles to yourself. To treat yourself like a dear friend worthy of love, nurturing and actionable support. This is the foundation of common humanity. The feelings and experience of suffering and pain are universal, regardless of subjective experiences. You enter entrapment when you isolate your experience to one of 'me' rather than 'we' or 'us'. Humans are not designed to overcome hardships on their own, yet, many suffer alone in silence.

Self-compassion is prioritised for heart energy renewal. The two pillars of self-compassion are:

• Loving-kindness in action
• Boundary setting

LOVING-KINDNESS IN ACTION

Self-compassion provides the comfort that may be absent from your current workplace, social community and family. The six stages of self-compassion in action are:

1. Observation: Observe your low energy state

'I acknowledge that I am not my usual self.'

2. Mindfulness: Be aware of the present moment

'In this moment, I am experiencing X.'

3. Common humanity: Recognise that suffering is universal and not unique to you

'Like others who have been through similar experiences, I recognise that I am human.'

4. Compassionate other: Adopt a nurturing tone (like that of a parent or kind friend)

'What would my compassionate other say to me in this moment? In what ways would they more delicately describe the realities of what is going on in this moment?'

5. Loving-kindness (also known as 'metta'): Connect with feelings of warmth

Placing both hands across your heart, close your eyes and repeat as many times as needed:

- *May I be safe.*
- *May I be free from suffering.*
- *May I be happy.*
- *May I be peaceful and at ease.*

6. Compassion towards others: Expand compassion outwards to someone in need of support

Repeat the words from step five, replacing 'I' with 'you':

- *May you be safe.*
- *May you be free from suffering.*
- *May you be happy.*
- *May you be peaceful and at ease.*

The practice of self-compassion is recommended on a daily basis or as you see fit. When you understand the importance of love and care better, you live and lead better.

In the book *Awakening Compassion at Work*, Monica Worline (a research scientist at Stanford University's Center for Compassion and Altruism Research and Education) and Jane Dutton (a university professor of business administration and psychology) explore whether compassion at work really matters:

> 'For employees who are under strain from deadlines or the stress of living up to performance demands, it's easy to forget that something that seems "soft" like compassion is significant. Facing challenges from turbulent environments, regulatory changes, or customer complaints, leaders and managers can easily dismiss the need for compassion. But when seeking to build high-performing organisations that meet the challenges of a twenty-first-century work environment, compassion matters more than most people recognise... Gallup researchers caution top leaders: "When compassion is called for, know that your bottom line is at stake".'

Compassion is, therefore, a human capability and strategic advantage for both individuals and organisations looking to thrive in the very place where they spend most of their waking hours.

BOUNDARY SETTING

Not only are boundaries an act of self-compassion, they are important to defuse workplace and social drama that are impacting your energy and wellbeing. Remember that during peak periods of change, more is being asked of you and your energy reserves, so guarding these reserves is essential.

When you are experiencing overwhelm and exhaustion, this is an indicator that your personal boundaries have been violated or that you have not installed any boundaries in the first instance. Boundaries can be either physical (your body and personal space) or emotional (your sense of identity and self-worth). Any time a boundary is violated, this is guaranteed to stir up negative feelings. When that occurs, check in with yourself to clearly define what the triggers are.

It is a waste of time to set boundaries if you are not going to stick to them. To do so requires clarity and communication. A lack of boundary setting can manifest as resentment and an inability to advocate for oneself and one's work. Boundary setting protects you from empathy or compassion fatigue. Compassion fatigue is referred to as the 'negative cost of care', where leading with heart and compassion ultimately weakens your emotional energy reserves if done to excess. Conversely, excessive boundary setting can result in a lack of vulnerability, which is a precursor to empathy and compassion. Effective and emotive change leadership is a delicate dance between the two.

In a *Forbes* article titled '10 Ways to Set Healthy Boundaries at Work', contributor Caroline Castrillon states, *'Employees who are the happiest and most productive are those who set boundaries. People who set limits gain respect because they show respect for themselves.'*

Holistic psychologist Dr. Nicole LePera refers to boundaries as the 'ultimate life hack', which 'give you space to protect your energy'.

She recommends you:

- Learn to say no and then step away, without justification or rationalisation.
- Prioritise your needs ahead of others', without the guilt or fear of repercussion.
- Know that with each 'no', the aftermath gets easier, so train yourself to keep going.
- Expect pushback and resistance. In that event, engage in self-compassion practices.

For example, let's say you have family responsibilities, which are visible in your work calendar for others to see. Then, without notice, you are given a revised timeline for a project that requires you to work through the night. Learn to say no in situations like this, knowing that the more times you define and articulate your boundaries, the less likely they'll be challenged in the future. Don't beat yourself up afterwards, either. Use that time to put your self-compassion practices into action.

Boundaries provide you with the space to regenerate and reconnect to your own unique energy. Boundaries build harmony, and harmony encourages optimism and opportunities to come your way. Tolerance for boundary breaches is common among those who were taught to 'be a good girl/boy', 'respect authority figures and elders', and 'toe the company/party line'. All of these mantras breed groupthink, conformism and co-dependency.

Boundaries define what you are willing to accept and not accept. Here's a brief outline of unhealthy boundaries versus healthy boundaries, and the difference in feelings and behaviours.

Unhealthy boundaries include:

- Giving away your power, leaving you feeling powerless.
- Giving away your energy, leaving you feeling exhausted.
- Giving away your identity, leaving you feeling incongruent.

Healthy boundaries include:

- Living in your power, whereby you are assertive, voice ideas and make impactful decisions.
- Living in your energy, whereby you wisely guard and conserve your energy for development.
- Living in your identity, whereby you are self-expressive and authentically you, inside and out.

Boundaries define your limitations in relation to others and to situations. Boundaries are your human right to protect and guard yourself. They signal 'no trespassing'.

Here are some key tips to building healthy boundaries:

- **Know your values:** Know your top three values and base all decisions off these.
- **Audit and reset boundaries:** Revisit and rebuild existing, weakened boundaries.
- **Honour boundaries:** If you don't, others won't either and you'll be forced to let them in.
- **Protect your boundaries:** Hold your ground by repeatedly saying no.

Stop running away from setting better boundaries. Self-integrity is everything. Be honest with yourself, stick to your word and walk your talk. Why? Because if you don't respect your boundaries, you are inviting others to violate them. Furthermore, if you don't honour your boundaries, this is a sure sign that self-respect and/or respect for others needs to be addressed.

As stated earlier, boundaries are crucial to defuse workplace and social drama. Drama may start externally but it lives on internally. In a TEDx Talk titled 'Ditch the drama', workplace drama researcher Cy Wakeman states that each person spends on average two and a half hours per day lost in drama. In addition to outwardly emotional displays, this includes the self-inflicted pain that comes with wrestling with your ego. Wakeman says:

> 'We suffer because of our stories, not because of our realities. What if you just stopped believing what you thought, and you paused and you self-reflected? This simple action lets you bypass your ego and taps into a better part of the brain.

> 'What would your life be like [if], instead of searching to be happier, and working so hard to be innovative, creative and engaged, you realised that you already were all those things? Once you've just chipped away all that [drama] that wasn't you. What if happiness and success is our natural state once the drama is gone?'

Wakeman recommends the following self-reflective questions to minimise 'emotional wastage' and 'rise above the conflict and have the impact you were born to have'.

- **When you are feeling judgemental**, ask 'What do I know for sure?'
  The focus is to change the story your ego has been telling you.
- **When you are feeling ego-fuelled**, ask 'What could I do to help?'
  The focus is to enhance rather than detract from the situation.
- **When you are feeling under siege**, ask 'What would great look like?'
  The focus is to succeed in spite of circumstances.

When thinking about boundaries, don't limit yourself to building up walls. Pause and self-reflect on your role in diffusing drama, too.

THE TRUE TEST

Our society is obsessed with short-term solutions and quick fixes that perpetuate busyness and the over-indexing of productivity. This means individuals are never given a chance to pause, slow down and truly regenerate. This leads to unresolved cycles of overwhelm, exhaustion and emotional suffering.

To successfully regenerate, you must learn how to disconnect from the daily grind and dive into the depths of your brain, body and mind using a multi-stage approach. It is only when you practise self-care and self-compassion that a deeper level of traction commences.

You have to put yourself first and heal the existing emotional trauma. You need to stop the mind and body reliving the initial or ongoing trauma by first alleviating the short-term panic, and then identifying and addressing the triggers and long-term stressors. Being forced to participate in a corporate fun run is not going to do this. Nor will a one-week wellness program.

You need to be intentional about your healing (short term) and habits (long term). When you are, you will:

- Calm the change chaos
- Appease the amygdala
- Soothe your nervous system
- Connect with your heart

Recognise all that it means to be a whole human. You owe it to yourself to be accountable for your intrapersonal growth. Don't allow time pressures, continuous change and competing demands to impact how you show up for yourself, your team and your loved ones.

CHAPTER SUMMARY

That brings us to the end of Chapter 4. By now, you should have a better understanding of what is meant by the phrase: 'The body keeps score.' Trauma awareness and appreciation provide a new dimension in which to interact with others with more empathy and compassion.

In Chapter 5, we'll discuss how to recode your mind. Before we dive into that, let's review the key points discussed in Chapter 4:

- Ground-breaking research, and specifically the release of the Polyvagal Theory by neuroscientist Dr. Stephen Porges, highlights how the body responds to, stores and retriggers trauma. Here's a recap:
  > Trauma is the fight/flight/freeze nervous system reaction trapped in an 'on' state.
  > Extreme stress can lead to 'self-preservation', whereby the body shuts down or freezes.
  > The Polyvagal Theory validates shutting down as a normalised response.
  > Neuroception is your nervous system subconsciously scanning for safety.
  > To overcome 'shutdown', the social engagement system needs to be activated.
  > The opposite of the 'freeze nerves' is the 'ease nerves', specifically the vagus nerve.
  > To stimulate the vagus nerve, practise breath work and the self-holding exercise.
  > Once safe from panic and trauma, focus on auditing your daily environments.

> Prioritise emotional safety and high-quality connections for you and your team.

- Mindful solitude is essential to the individual regeneration process, which includes:
  > Self-care (sleep prioritisation and fear minimisation)
  > Self-compassion (loving-kindness in action and boundary setting)

In a fast-paced world, crashing, resting and slowing down is essential to your emotional and physical wellbeing. You can't survive by striving your way out. You need to be deliberate in integrating regeneration into all facets of your life.

CHAPTER 5

RECODE YOUR MIND

'It is difficult to make a man miserable while he feels worthy of himself.'
– ABRAHAM LINCOLN

The 1992 movie *A Few Good Men* is a dramatic courtroom thriller about the defence of two U.S. Marines accused of murdering a colleague. The storyline centres on whether PFC Santiago, the victim, was given a 'code red'.

In the beginning of the movie, we are introduced to a brash Navy lawyer who is known for being lazy and looking for the easy way out of difficult cases. True to form, he files a plea bargain. However, the accused's aunt is convinced that there is more to the story, so the legal team succumbs to exploring the case in greater detail and, in the process, uncovers case-cracking information.

At the conclusion of the movie (spoiler alert!), emotions in the courtroom are at an all-time high as Lieutenant Daniel Kaffee, the Navy lawyer (played by Tom Cruise), interrogates Colonel Nathan Jessup (Jack Nicholson) about the ordering of the code red. This brings us to the infamous scene where Jessup is irate at being caught in a lie that had covered up the murder.

Next, Kaffee attempts to exploit Jessup's brazenness when it comes to the Marines. Jessup emotionally explodes and extols the military's importance, and his own, to national security. The scene closes with Kaffee demanding to know if he ordered the code red and Jessup blatantly admitting perjury with the line, '*You're God damn right I did.*'

As the saying goes, knowledge is power. However, when knowledge is coupled with human emotion and core beliefs, this is when real power (right or wrong) actualises. Surviving endless change in today's workplace is no easy feat. If it were, more people would be thriving in their jobs and energised at the prospect of the future of work.

In earlier chapters, I showcased how primal thoughts dominate your mind. Specifically, self-preservation, belonging and safety. To overcome this, you need to engage in methods such as self-care and self-compassion. This chapter requires a deeper level of personal development that hinges upon self-insight, self-assessment and self-acceleration. The key objective is to help you recode your brain and master your mind for change at the belief or identity level. The focus here is on long-lasting, sustainable change rather than a quick fix. First and foremost, this means shifting your focus from 'bouncing back' to 'bouncing forward'.

BOUNCING FORWARD

Right now, you are at a choice point. You have to decide whether bouncing back from overwhelm, change fatigue and burnout is enough for you, or whether you are eager to self-extend beyond that. A common misperception is that the ability to bounce back from adversity is the peak outcome.

What if there were an alternative? Bouncing forward! If you are still battle-scarred and experiencing low energy, then this may sound like an impossible reality. However, what I am talking about here is not piling on more action steps and activities (the kind that deplete you), but rather zoning in on your future aspirations (the kind that energise you).

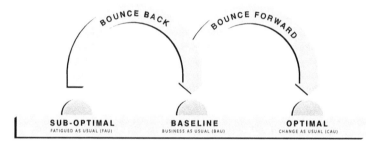

Figure 7: Bouncing forward.

Bouncing back means building resilience that returns you to your previous set-point. Bouncing forward means building resilience beyond your previous set-point. Psychologists refer to the latter as post-traumatic growth (PTG). Post-traumatic growth is the experience of aligning new meaning and positive change post trauma.

This topic was explored by Facebook's COO Sheryl Sandberg and Wharton management and psychology professor Adam Grant after the death of Sandberg's husband. Their book, *Option B: Facing Adversity, Building Resilience, and Finding Joy*, explores PTSD, the cycle of grief and the ripple effects of resilience afterwards.

They write:

> 'Many of these [trauma victims] experienced ongoing anxiety and depression. Still, along with these negative emotions there were some positive changes. Up to that point, psychologists had focused mostly on two possible outcomes of trauma. Some people struggled: They developed PTSD, faced debilitating depression and anxiety or had difficulty functioning. Others were resilient: They bounced back to their state before the trauma. Now there was a third possibility: People who suffered could bounce forward.'

Sheryl goes on to say:

> '... I thought resilience was the capacity to endure pain, so I asked Adam how I could figure out how much I had. He explained that our amount of resilience isn't fixed, so I should be asking instead how I could become resilient. Resilience is the strength and speed of our response to adversity – and we can build it. It isn't about having a backbone. It's about strengthening the muscles around our backbone.'

A key insight here is the notion that blame delays recovery. In addition to that, I believe that the difference between bouncing back and bouncing forward is learning about the facets of your mind and the role they play in supporting or hindering your success.

RECODE BRIEFING: MIND THEORIES AND MODELS

The seed of all resistance, and, therefore, change, resides within the subconscious mind. Only when this is adequately addressed can you expect change to deliver the desired short-term and, more importantly, long-term outcomes. For deep change to be welcomed in and stick, you must look within and optimally recode or reprogram yourself.

Let's now explore a selection of mind theories and models, including:

- Theory of the unconscious
- Ericksonian hypnosis
- Power of your subconscious mind
- Quantum model of reality

Remember that the following are glimmers into rather in-depth works that should be further explored, should they pique your interest.

I. THEORY OF THE UNCONSCIOUS

In 1921, psychiatrist and psychologist Carl Jung published *Psychology of the Unconscious*. Jung is also rather famous for disagreeing with and 'unfriending' Sigmund Freud over the meaning of dreams. Jung did not agree with Freud's claim that your dreams are a reflection of your 'repressed sexual desire'. Instead, Jung believed that your dreams are a bridge to the unconscious or subconscious mind and its creative abilities. Jung also supported the notion that patients and therapists work best in a face-to-face, collaborative manner to shape outcomes. In analytical psychology, the key elements of the psyche, as defined by the theory of the unconscious, are:

Ego
This is your conscious mind. Your awareness of your thoughts, emotions and memories. This also includes your level of introversion and extroversion.

Personal unconscious
This is the storehouse of information in your mind that is not 'readily available'. Examples include repressed memories, traumatic experiences and charged emotions known as 'complexes'.

Collective unconscious
Sometimes referred to as the 'objective psyche', this is your genetically inherited or 'inborn' unconscious mind. This infers that ancestors passed down primal instincts and beliefs.

Archetypes
This is part of the collective unconscious, and symbolises your inner personalities and motivations. This includes a) personas (masks), b) shadows (darker instincts), and c) anima or animus (the true self).

Jung stated, *'I am not what happened to me, I am what I choose to become.'* The essence of his work is designed to help you reveal your *true self* and lead a fulfilling life.

Key insights
There are two key points to remember here. The first that your

behaviour is not solely determined by your past experiences. Rather, it is a combination of your past experiences, genetic inheritance and your future aspirations. Being able to articulate your future aspirations is key. The second key point is that self-work is best described as peeling away the layers of an onion. For example, identifying which personas or beliefs are no longer serving you, and replacing them with your future, upgraded aspirations.

2. ERICKSONIAN HYPNOSIS

Psychologist, psychiatrist and 'godfather of hypnotherapy' Dr Milton Erickson shot to fame within his field when a former student published his work in *Uncommon Therapy* in 1973. In line with the expression 'necessity is the mother of invention', Erickson taught himself self-hypnosis to minimise and manage the pain of polio at age seventeen.

Erickson's model of the mind is present focused, with the model and associated methods being process based. This is a similar construct to how business consultants map out workflow and tasks for process improvement and business efficiencies. Erickson would first build rapport with the patient, and then listen to the language and sequence (the process) replaying over and over in their mind each day. Only once the process was specified could he 'pattern-interrupt' (break the ingrained sequence of that process). The key elements of Ericksonian hypnosis are:

Indirect suggestion

The subconscious mind is highly responsive to indirect suggestion, which includes the extensive use of metaphors and storytelling (similar to how this book is designed). This is a less forceful, gentler tone of language, designed to build rapport and induce relaxation.

It's particularly useful for patients (and anyone!) with anxious tendencies.

Trances

Daydreaming, and being lost in your thoughts, best describes everyday trances. Here, the subconscious mind takes the wheel of control. For example, imagine you are driving home and don't remember the specifics of how you got there. You were on auto-pilot, thanks to your subconscious taking control of the wheel. Through the induction process, patients are able to go into deeper levels of trance for clinical subconscious work.

Legacy

The founders of neuro-linguistic programming (NLP), Richard Bandler and John Grinder, modelled NLP off the work of Milton Erickson (hypnotherapy), Virginia Satir (family therapy) and Fritz Perls (gestalt therapy). On his blog, Dr. Michael Yapko, a clinical psychologist and fellow of the American Psychological Association, credits Erickson's work as being the 'original positive psychology' back in the 1940s, stating that clinical hypnosis acts as a vehicle to put 'positive psychology in practice'.

Key insights

There are two key points to remember here. Firstly, the founding premise of hypnosis is that it only works if the patient wants it to. Otherwise, the critical faculty will not be bypassed. Think of the critical faculty as your judgement filter, which has evolved from your upbringing and education. It is designed to block or filter out unwanted suggestions that are not aligned with your beliefs. However, it is prone to error and this means that beneficial suggestions may also be blocked. This is where the feeling of 'stuckness' or feeling 'blocked' surfaces. It is your conscious awareness of this inner defence mechanism that you will address in coaching or self-directed coaching to become a Change Optimiser.

Research by Alfred Barrios, laid out in *Psychology and Psychotherapy: Theory, Research and Practice*, tested and validated the effectiveness of hypnotherapy (ninety-three per cent success rate after six sessions) in comparison to psychotherapy (thirty-eight per cent success rate after 600 sessions).

The second key point to remember is that, similar to mental health, there remains a stigma associated with clinical hypnosis. However, in its simplest terms, clinical hypnosis can be thought of as process-based, guided meditation that bypasses the critical faculty and focuses on a future-oriented goal. Later in the chapter, we will explore ways to kick-start the process yourself, right from the comfort of your own home.

3. POWER OF YOUR SUBCONSCIOUS MIND

In 1963, Dr. Joseph Murphy published *The Power of Your Subconscious Mind*. The central premise is to remove subconscious obstacles and focus your mind on what you really do want in order to achieve success in your life. Murphy is known for influencing Tony Robbins, Zig Ziglar and Earl Nightingale. Here's a couple of the key concepts discussed in the book:

Law of your mind

This is your belief in belief itself. *'Psychologists and psychiatrists point out that when thoughts are conveyed to your subconscious mind, impressions are made in the brain cells. As soon as your subconscious mind accepts any idea, it proceeds to put it into effect immediately.*

It works by association of ideas and uses every bit of knowledge
that you have gathered in your lifetime to bring about its purpose.'

Infinite intelligence

This is your ability to stop accepting 'false thoughts' and write
new code for all that you want to achieve, the goals you wish to
reach and the legacy you intend to leave behind you.

Key insights

There are two key points to remember here. The first is to visualise your goals every day, maintaining a 'can do' attitude. Replace
fears with positive, success-inducing thoughts. You already possess the tools to do this; you just need to use them. The second
key point is to feed your mind with high-value content for your
personal development, passion and career. Focus on your change
capability and goals that will be truly fulfilling and of service to
your community, too.

4. QUANTUM MODEL OF REALITY

In 2012, Dr. Joe Dispenza, a global expert in 'the biology of change',
released the book *Breaking the Habit of Being Yourself: How to Lose*
Your Mind and Create a New One. This work is designed to be a
bridge between true human potential and neuroplasticity. Here
is how Dr. Dispenza defines his model:

> *'The quantum model of reality tells us that to change our lives,*
> *we must fundamentally change the ways we think, act, and*
> *feel. We must change our state of being. Because how we think,*
> *feel, and behave is, in essence, our personality, it is our per-*
> *sonality that creates our personal reality. So to create a new*
> *personal reality, a new life, we must create a new personality;*

we must become someone else. To change, then, is to think and act greater than our present circumstances, greater than our environment.'

Dr. Dispenza also states, *'95% of who we are by the time we're 35 years old, is a memorised set of behaviours, emotional reactions, unconscious habits, hardwired attitudes, beliefs and perceptions that function like a computer program.'*

Please be aware that the following terms are interchangeable: learning and relearning, wiring and rewiring, programming and reprogramming, and coding and recoding. Here is how Dr. Dispenza defines the subconscious mind and the conscious mind:

Subconscious mind

Your subconscious mind develops, or is programmed, from in-utero up until the age of around seven or eight. During this time, your brain waves cycle between the slower alpha and theta brain waves, which is a similar state to light trance, hypnosis and meditation. If you were a child of the eighties, this is comparable to putting a blank cassette in a cassette player and pressing the record button, storing not just the direct information but all of the indirect information, too. The subconscious mind equates to ninety-five per cent of your total mind and is responsible for foundational beliefs, habits and behaviours. In essence, your identity is greatly influenced by those around you (parents, teachers, schools, social groups and so on).

Conscious mind

The conscious mind equates to five per cent of your total mind and is responsible for logic, reasoning, willpower, morality and faith. When your willpower runs out, which it does when fatigued and stressed, you default to your foundational beliefs to keep you safe. For example, when your willpower is depleted due to exhaustion, your ability to uphold your corporate mask and to enact best practices defaults to what feels easy and habitual even though it may not be as integral. Let's say one belief you hold is that seeing tasks through is linked to your identity and, therefore, you self-identify as a 'completionist'. In the event that willpower is depleted, you will cut corners that you usually wouldn't to get the job done. This impacts the quality of your work and, ultimately, your personal brand.

Key insights
There are two key points to remember here. The first is that the only way to change or recode your subconscious programs or beliefs is to bypass the more critical, conscious mind and access the subconscious mind. Clinical hypnosis and self-directed neuroplasticity are the gateway into the theta brain wave state. The second key point is that the theta state naturally occurs during the first eight minutes of waking up, and again at night just before you 'nod off' to sleep. This will be explored further later in the chapter.

Now that you have a foundational introduction to the inner workings of your mind, there are three elements to fast-track the recoding:

- Self-insight (blind spot awareness)
- Self-assessment (state and stake awareness)
- Self-acceleration (theta state and theta hacking awareness)

Let's discuss each of those elements in more detail, starting with self-insight.

SELF-INSIGHT

Blind spot awareness is the first key to self-insight. Here is a selection of blind spots that you need to be aware of in order to avoid self-sabotage and be at ease with change:

- Your ego and the need to be right, which closes you off
- Your biases, which poison your perspective
- Your emotions, which exacerbate everything
- Your low self-worth, which limits your potential

Let's discuss each of those blind spots in more detail.

BLIND SPOT #I: YOUR NEED TO BE RIGHT CLOSES YOU OFF

The need to be right is intrinsically linked to your belief system within your subconscious mind. It is also reinforced by society. Let's look at reasons why you are hooked on 'being right':

- It appeases society's need for accuracy. This premise has been conditioned by your parents, the education system and the workplace that accrues value from your expertise.
- It appeases alphas. This verbally positions your assertiveness and authority. Eckhart Tolle describes the need to be right as a form of violence (in a psychological sense).
- It appeases expectations – both the ones placed on you by others and the ones you place on yourself.
- It appeases the ego. The series of mini wins and accompanying positive self-talk – like 'I'm right' or 'There – I've had the last word' – are accompanied by dopamine rewards.

In *The Power of Now*, Eckhart Tolle sums it up well by writing:

> 'There is nothing that strengthens the ego more than being right. Being right is identification with a mental position – a perspective, an opinion, a judgement, a story. For you to be right of course, you need someone else to be wrong, and so the ego loves to make wrong in order to be right. In other words: You need to make others wrong in order to get a stronger sense of who you are. Not only a person, but a situation can be made wrong through complaining and reactivity, which always implies that "this should not be happening". Being right places you in a position of imagined moral superiority in relation to the person or situation that is being judged and found wanting.'

The wrong side of needing to be right is that:

- It closes off humility and servant leadership.
- It closes off your ability to mindfully listen to others.
- It closes off your ability to receive new ideas.
- It closes off your creative flow (this will be explored in the final chapter).

Here are some simple ways to get over your need to be right:

- Recognise that it is a limiting egoic pattern (name and shame it).
- Have verbal responses at the ready for times of need (respond with 'okay' or nothing).
- Be open to accepting or at least listening to others' views (stay flexible and at ease).
- Practise self-compassion during new habit forming (proceed slowly but steadily).

BLIND SPOT #2: YOUR BIASES POISON YOUR PERSPECTIVE

All humans suffer from cognitive biases. Biases impair rational judgement, decision making and problem solving in social and workplace scenarios. According to a McKinsey & Company article titled 'The business logic in debiasing', *'Debiasing business decision making has drawn board-level attention, as companies doing it are achieving marked performance improvements.'*

A McKinsey survey of nearly 800 board members and chairpersons revealed that 'reducing decision biases' is their number-one aspiration for improving performance. This research reinforces the fact that prioritising bias awareness, and debiasing programs at an individual and organisational level, is critical to reducing the associated negative effects. These include a decline in profits, productivity and employee engagement, to name a few.

According to Wikipedia, there are over 175 biases! Let's now look at a selection of biases that may prove useful as you endeavour to recode your mind for optimal change:

Affective forecasting
You tend to predict that how you will feel in the future will match how you feel now. For example, if you are on the brink of burnout now, it is likely that you can't foresee how you could possibly be in a different state in the future.

Pessimism bias
You tend to overestimate the likelihood of negative things happening to you in the future. For example, let's say you are advised that, due to a restructure, you are going to have to report to a

new leader. You instantly believe this will have an adverse effect.

Negativity bias

You tend to recall unpleasant memories and experiences more than positive ones. The evolutionary purpose of being hardwired for negativity is to keep you safe in the future. Here, the expression 'once bitten, twice shy' rings true.

Normalcy bias

You tend to underestimate the possible effects of a disaster taking place. For example, as a leader, you may be at risk of underestimating the impact of burnout from organisational change. You tell yourself, 'I'll think about the consequences later.'

Status quo bias

You tend to have an emotional bias towards things staying the same. For example, you may not understand the need for change and business transformation. You might say, 'There's nothing wrong with the way things are done around here.'

Loss aversion bias

You tend to estimate the pain of loss twice as much as the pleasure of gains. For example, you experience twice as much negative emotion after hearing you will lose your fixed desk to hot-desking, even though the benefits of hot-desking have been outlined.

Unconscious bias

You hold unconscious beliefs about social stereotypes that results in categorising. For example, your decision to hire a new team member solely because they suit the workplace culture is a form of similarity bias that can result in groupthink.

Bandwagon effect
You tend to do (or believe) things because many other people believe the same. For example, as more team members begin to trial and adopt a new technology, you are more likely to follow suit and hop on the bandwagon, too.

Curse of knowledge
When you are better informed, you find it extremely difficult to think about problems from the perspective of lesser-informed people. For example, the executive team may underestimate the level of overwhelm experienced by junior staff.

Black-and-white thinking
You tend to claim there are only 'either/or' or two alternatives available. Psychologists refer to this polarisation as 'splitting'. In essence, you cannot find a rational middle ground and, thus, default to one of two extreme ends.

IKEA effect
You place a disproportionately high value on products or initiatives that you partially created, such as furniture from IKEA. For example, if you co-create a change initiative, you are more likely to be invested in the outcome.

Attentional bias
Your perception tends to be influenced by recurring thoughts. For example, if you are ruminating about how you are going to cope with more stress, this will limit your openness to different perspectives about what the future will hold.

Fundamental attribution error

You tend to internally judge a person's character or personality based on their (negative) behaviour, rather than taking into account the situational factors. For example, a tardy employee is automatically viewed as lazy.

By now, you may be starting to realise that it is human nature to think and behave irrationally due to cognitive biases. So how can you de-bias yourself? It's a two-step process:

1. Build your self-awareness so that you recognise when a bias is in play.
2. Actively choose to disarm or course-correct this yourself by using the power of the pause in the first instance. Slow down to recognise the situation and present cognitive bias in the moment, not in hindsight. Some of you may opt to print out a cheat sheet and place it in your compendium or pin it up on your office wall for quick reference.

As *Monkey Mind* author Daniel Smith puts it, *'This is why therapists go to such lengths to urge their anxious patients away from intellectualisation: The first step toward peace is disarmament.'*

BLIND SPOT #3: YOUR EMOTIONS EXACERBATE EVERYTHING

Emotions provide powerful data about your inner 'energy in motion'. Change becomes more human when it is recognised as an 'inside job'. Tapping into your emotions, your beliefs and your identity is not something that can be engineered by consultants. It's a flawed assumption that it can be done from the top down or from social herding. This becomes clear when you repeatedly hear that seventy per cent of large-scale change initiatives fail to meet their long-term goals.

Emotional intelligence allows you to become consciously aware of your underlying emotions as they arise across the day. You may consider actively tracking the following limiting and liberating change emotions to determine whether you have a dominant limiting change emotion that requires your attention.

Limiting change emotions
- Fear drives fight-or-flight responses and self-preservation
- Anger drives resistance and self-protection
- Sadness drives a sense of lacking and loss

Liberating change emotions
- Compassion drives you to actively support others
- Curiosity drives you to explore, enquire and learn
- Passion drives creativity and innovation

BLIND SPOT #4: YOUR LOW SELF-WORTH LIMITS YOUR POTENTIAL

In earlier chapters, I briefly touched on the notion of self-esteem. As a recap, self-esteem is a contextual-based feeling that arises within. It is fleeting rather than fixed. Self-worth, on the other hand, is linked to your identity. It is a constant baseline that accompanies you. Self-worth gives you the freedom to strive. Not only to strive, but to strive and fail – and feel good about your efforts in doing so. When you stop defining yourself by other people's opinions, you have the space to ideate, create and innovate. Self-worth, therefore, precedes external psychological safety.

Goal attainment has been replaced by value creation and outcome delivery. Self-worth is, therefore, the secret to your success because it will empower you to back yourself, be more decisive and voice your opinion. Why? Because when you have high self-worth and feel energised, you become unstoppable. Societal handcuffs melt away and you begin to see or carve out new opportunities for yourself and those around you.

Having high self-worth is akin to sitting inside the Melbourne Cricket Ground (MCG) during footy season. Rain, hail or shine, the match goes ahead. You know that you will be safe and protected within the walls of the solid architecture. Even among a crowd of 80,000 roaring fans, you feel that you belong. Not only that, but your decision to cheer on your team could boost their spirits and help them win the game, even when they are physically spent.

Your self-worth is the same. When it is unshakeable, you are unshakeable. When it has your back, you keep pushing through the internal barriers (your mind) and external barriers (your environment) of change. In contrast, when you have experienced burnout, you feel stripped bare. The voices in the stands have gone quiet and you feel alone in the aftermath, wondering if you will ever return to your former glory.

How you define yourself in this moment is your self-worth. Your opinions either reflect insecurities and limiting beliefs or self-worth.

Limiting beliefs in action
- Am I good enough?
- Do I have the capacity?
- Are others going to judge me?

Low self-worth in action

- I rely on others.
- I find problems with everything.
- I feel like everything and everyone are against me.

High self-worth in action

- I've got this.
- I am free to explore this further.
- I am worth the effort.

This has been extended in the following 'self-worth snapshot':

SELF-WORTH SNAPSHOT		
SENSES	SPECIFICS	STEPS
Sounds like (internal dialogue)	I have and will continue to overcome personal and professional road-blocks and struggles.	Pausing to hear your mind's negative chatter. When you tune into it, it will be present.
	I'm not shackled by yesterday's thinking. I tell myself a different, more hopeful story.	Removing any language that is blocking you from success. It is always easier to cut it out than add to it.
	I am capable of changing my environment, mindset and energy. I am wholeheartedly accountable.	Coaching yourself in a way that builds your confidence. For example, 'What if I gave myself permission to...?'
	I bring intrinsic value to the world, exactly as I stand in this present moment. My value is always evolving.	Learning and evolving every day via increments, losses and wins.

SELF-WORTH SNAPSHOT		
SENSES	SPECIFICS	STEPS
Feels like (kinaesthetic feedback)	I have accepted that as a human being I have flaws, fears and failures, and will continue to be okay knowing that.	Checking in with your body to get a sense for what feels authentic rather than what feels right. The difference is in the subtlety.
	I am at ease and mentally unrestrained by the past (it is done) or the future (uncertainties are inevitably infinite). My focus is now.	Focusing in on the moments that matter. Leaning in to raw emotions and tough times, and finding the learnings in adversity.
	I feel empowered by not allowing others to disempower me via coercive or co-dependent measures.	Learning to notice gut feeling or intuition dramatically speeds up decision making.
	I am non-defensive when my ideas, my work and my presence is questioned or critiqued by others.	Reaching out to those who harmonise and energise you to connect, contribute and co-create.
Looks like (external physiology)	I stand proud in who I am and in who I am becoming.	Remembering that your physiology is informed by your psychology.
	I have a presence that is contextually appropriate and not shrinking, anxious or depressed.	Avoiding displays of toxic positivity. When positivity is falsified or magnified, others become less trusting of you.

SELF-WORTH SNAPSHOT		
SENSES	SPECIFICS	STEPS
Looks like (external physiology)	I am visibly refreshed and energised the majority of the time.	Practising power posing (space-expanding hands on hips pose), voice projection and eye contact.
	I am lit up with hope, optimism and new, creative ideas.	Seeking out stillness to address any resistance to brainstorming and creating.

By prioritising your self-worth, you're more likely to:

- Reframe the baseline perception you have of yourself. Everything hinges off this!
- Rebuild trust with your intuition once your needs have been met.
- Reinstall positive feelings towards yourself as well as others.
- Rediscover how to freely experiment and continuously change without fear of failure.

SELF-ASSESSMENT

Let's keep this part short and sweet. An optimal change outcome requires you to balance both your *state in the outcome* and your *stake in the outcome*. Allow me to explain what I mean by that...

STATE IN THE OUTCOME: YOUR INTERNAL EMOTIONAL EXPERIENCE

Your state in the outcome is largely unable to be influenced by others. This is dependent on your commitment to embrace change at the intrinsic motivation level. Your current state of mind, under-pinned by your beliefs, is what will drive your behaviours. In other words, will you psychologically 'lean in' to change or lean out? Are you identifying as Change Capable?

STAKE IN THE OUTCOME: YOUR EXTERNAL CONTRIBUTION

Your stake in the outcome is able to be influenced by others to the extent to which they openly communicate, collaborate and co-create the design and delivery of change initiatives. In other words, whether you creatively contribute and whether this contribution is viewed as valuable by the organisation, based on its culture.

PAUSE & REFLECT

- Self-assess both your state and stake in a recent change outcome.
- You may prefer to do this by ranking your experience and contribution (from, say, zero to five), or by writing down your thoughts before comparing the state/stake pair.

SELF-ACCELERATION

In this section, we'll explore two elements of self-acceleration: reticular activating system (RAS) reliance and theta 'brain wave' hacking.

RAS RELIANCE

When the poet Rumi tells you to 'live as if everything is rigged in your favour', she is onto a winner here. With this in mind, I want you to turn your focus to the reticular activating system (RAS). This part of the brain is designed to filter out information that is less relevant or important so that you can keep your focus elsewhere. The most obvious example is when you are at a crowded party and you hear your name across the room. No, your ears were not burning – you can thank your RAS. This is referred to as cocktail party phenomenon. Another example is when you are learning to drive and suddenly you notice all the other learner drivers on the road.

So, when it comes to goal setting, activating this area of the brain can make all of the difference, largely because all of your senses (except smell) are wired directly to this bundle of neurons. This allows the information into your conscious mind and activates the emotional brain. It's like a bouncer letting you into a nightclub and then ushering you to the VIP section. This is where the meeting of the minds (the conscious mind and the subconscious mind) convene over your intentions.

Learning about self-directed neuroplasticity and the reticular activating system supports the premise that recoding your mind is within your reach. In her book *The Source: The Secrets of the Universe, the Science of the Brain*, neuroscientist and university lecturer Dr. Tara Swart writes about mental resilience, adversity capability and the science behind why the law of attraction is a reality. In other words, that positive thinking perpetuates positive outcomes and vice versa.

According to Swart, *'most of the things we want from life—health, happiness, wealth, love—are governed by our ability to think, feel, and act; in other words, by our brain.'* *The Source* goes on to outline six key areas in relation to this:

Abundance
When you negate scarcity in exchange for abundance, you prime your brain towards positivity and positive outcomes. This releases the happiness neurochemical, oxytocin. For example, you can switch your narrative from 'I can't cope' to 'I am resilient'.

Manifestation
The Source clearly articulates this is beyond just thinking. Rather, it is persistent perseverance to turn your dream into a reality. It combines thoughts with feelings with actions. Think of it as a triple threat.

Magnetic desire
This is your inner belief that your change goals or future aspirations are already a reality and absolutely within your grasp. This comes down to the strength of your conviction, which allows you to tap into the emotional limbic system.

Patience
You need to repeat magnetic desire to slowly and surely strengthen the neural paths. This takes time and grit – do not give up prematurely and waste the initial effort.

Harmony

Harmony refers to your ability to align the executive, emotional and gut brain. Focus on stress optimisation, emotional resilience and probiotic consumption. For example, don't overstretch yourself, be kind to yourself and follow a healthy diet.

Universal connection (to others)

Focus on belonging and making meaningful contributions to social groups. Focus on high-quality relationships and connections; cut all toxicity (people, places and things).

Now you know *how* to recode your mind, let's talk about *when* the optimal time is to do it.

THETA HACKING

The subconscious mind is responsible for the energy and alignment of your beliefs. If you don't want the result, you won't get the result. If you can't see your future self living the result, it is never going to happen. The role of theta hacking (accessing the subconscious mind) is to help you visualise your realised success.

Most people try to push through using desperation tactics, which don't work at the eleventh hour because you are still operating in the sub-optimal mode of fight or flight. When cortisol is pumping around your body, you are the least open and malleable to change. Your body and mind are primed to protect, charge and fight. The polar opposite of this state is referred to as theta state, where your brain is so deeply relaxed that it's malleable.

The following table outlines the brain wave states:

BRAIN WAVE STATES	DEPTH OF MIND	ELEMENTS
Gamma waves Frequency: 30 Hz & above	Peak focus/flow Examples include the hyper-focused breakthroughs when scientists, musicians and athletes are 'in the zone'.	High-level cognition, expanded conscious-ness and memory recall. Links to exceptional intelligence, and high levels of self-control and self-compassion.
Beta waves Frequency: 13 to 30 Hz	Conscious mind Examples include every-day functioning at your job.	Fully awake, active and alert. Activates consciousness, concen-tration and learning.
Alpha waves Frequency: 8 to 13 Hz	Gateway to subcon-scious mind Examples include winding down for bed, or tapping into your imagination with a good book.	Eyes closing, and you are relaxed, calm and not thinking. Activates daydreaming, relaxation and reflection.
Theta waves Frequency: 4 to 8 Hz	Subconscious mind Examples include common trance states like driving home on autopilot, children zoned in to video games and hot coal walkers.	Deeply relaxed state, used in hypnosis, deep meditation and REM (rapid eye movement) sleep. Activates dreaming, uninhibited creativity and mental clarity.
Delta waves Frequency: 0.1 to 4 Hz	Unconscious mind Examples include when a patient is under anaesthetic.	Deep sleep, dreamless slumber, automatic self-healing, immune system functioning.

There are two ways to access your subconscious mind. The first is deep meditation. I'm not talking about run-of-the-mill, basic meditation here. This requires Zen master teacher training and hours upon hours to truly tap into it. It is the biggest myth of the wellness industry that meditation is relaxing and successful for everyone. For the undisciplined and most chronically stressed individuals, it has the opposite effect of being anxiety-inducing. It can prompt thoughts like, 'I just can't seem to relax,' 'The thoughts are still racing in my mind,' and 'Why is this not coming easily to me?'

The second way to access your subconscious is through hypnosis, either via self-hypnosis (theta hacking) or clinical hypnotherapy with an accredited professional. As the name implies, theta hacking taps into the theta brain waves where the subconscious mind is accessible. There are two naturally occurring windows of opportunity to theta hack, both of which last around eight minutes:

- Pre-slumber brain wave state (the nodding off state)
- Post-slumber brain wave state (the waking state)

During this time, you should avoid reaching for your smartphone (or tablet or laptop) and scrolling news sites or social media. Rather than allow your malleable brain to be imprinted by low-value content, leverage this window of opportunity for high-value content. For example, dedicate this time to meditation, journaling, writing out goals, writing out what you are grateful for or reading a book of significance for your personal development. This is your opportunity to minimise fear and anxiety, and replace it with promise

and possibility. Pro tip: Journal the same three sentence openers to build brain familiarity with the practice. For example:
'I am grateful for...'
'I am cultivating this emotion towards myself and others...'
'I am laser-focused on...'

In a *Fast Company* article titled 'How to Hack Your Brain for Creative Ideas Before You Even Get Out Of Bed', author Kate Rodriguez quotes Ned Herrmann (who has developed models of brain activity and integrated them into teaching and management training):

> 'During this awakening cycle it is possible for individuals to stay in the theta state for an extended period of say, five to fifteen minutes – which would allow them to have a free flow of ideas about yesterday's events or to contemplate the activities of the forthcoming day. This time can be extremely productive and can be a period of very meaningful and creative mental activity.'

So be sure to 'bookend' your day with theta hacking for recoding success. The payoff of recoding your mind for success – in your job and beyond – results in a noted shift from inherited traits to inherent traits. The differences are outlined in the following table.

INHERITED TRAITS (LASTING NEGATIVE CONSEQUENCES)	INHERENT TRAITS (LASTING POSITIVE CONSEQUENCES)
Pre-programming (observational settings)	Recoding (success settings)
Identity defining (fixed)	Identity evolving (fluid)
Negative, limiting beliefs	Positive, liberating beliefs
Conformant, compliant, co-dependent	Accountable, committed, independent

THE POWER OF ONE

Changes to your subconscious mind and your identity rarely happen overnight. Regardless of your journey and the energy required to recode your mind, phenomenal change is within your reach. Once the inner game is strengthened, this has the power to ripple out and influence others. Remember that movements start one individual – rather than one leader – at a time.

In the TED Talk titled 'How to start a movement', Derek Sivers dissects what it takes to start a movement by analysing a crowd at a music festival. It starts with 'one lone nut' dancing enthusiastically by himself to the music. This is followed by two turning points. The first turning point is when the first follower shows up to join in the enthusiastic dancing. The initial dancer welcomes him as an equal and this escalates his status to leader. Feeling safe and valued, the first follower calls for his friend to rise up and join in the movement. Before too long, a full crowd of followers confirms the movement. At the end of the talk, Sivers highlights the lessons from this:

'So first, if you are the type, like the shirtless dancing guy that is standing alone, remember the importance of nurturing your first few followers as equals so it's clearly about the movement, not you.

'The biggest lesson, if you noticed – did you catch it? – is that leadership is over-glorified. Yes, it was the shirtless guy who was first, and he'll get all the credit, but it was really the first follower that transformed the lone nut into a leader. So, as we're told that we should all be leaders, that would be really *ineffective. If you really care about starting a movement, have the courage to follow and show others how to follow.'*

In the next chapter, you will shift your attention to ways in which you can accelerate your creative contribution through greater participation in value creation.

CHAPTER SUMMARY

That brings us to the end of Chapter 5. By now, you should have a clearer understanding of the mind/brain relationship. In a nutshell, the brain is like the hard drive of a computer; the mind is like the software in that it is able to be updated or recoded. Don't let an inherited virus limit your change potential. The key question posed is this: Now you know you are *able*, are you *willing* to recode and evolve?

In Chapter 6, we'll discuss the importance of imagination, creativity and tapping into the flow state. Before we dive into that, let's review the key points discussed in Chapter 5:

- Mind theories vary in terms of components and the significance of those components within your mind. The four examples briefly explored were:
  - > Theory of the unconscious
  - > Ericksonian hypnosis
  - > Power of your subconscious mind
  - > Quantum model of reality

- Recoding is able to be fast-tracked via:
  - > Self-insight (blind spot awareness)
  - > Self-assessment (state and stake awareness)
  - > Self-acceleration (theta state and theta hacking awareness)

- There are two key times of the day when theta hacking is available to you – when you're in the pre-slumber brain wave state (the nodding off state) and the post-slumber brain wave state (the waking state).

- When you recode your mind, this has the power to ripple out and influence others. All it takes is one individual (you!) to start a movement.

CHAPTER 6

REIMAGINE YOUR CREATIVITY

*'You often feel tired, not because you've
done too much, but because you've done
too little of what sparks a light in you.'*

– ALEXANDER DEN HEIJER

T
he movie *Life Is Beautiful* remains one of the highest gross-
ing foreign movies ever made. At the start of the movie,
which is set in 1939, an Italian Jew named Guido (played
by Robert Benigni) is first introduced to gentile Dora (played
by Nicoletta Braschi), who happens to be engaged to a fascist.
Through a series of comedic coincidences, Guido, a modern-day
clown, eventually wins Dora's heart. This results in a marriage
and the birth of their son.

The second half of the movie fast forwards to 1945, near the end
of the war. Starkly, Guido and his son are taken away to a concentration camp. Dora begs to go with them in a naive and desperate
attempt to stay close to her husband and son. At the concentration camp, Guido relies on his signature strength, his vivid

imagination, to protect his son from the truth. As the German guards are shouting harsh orders, Guido translates what is being said into an alternative narrative that sparks curiosity in his son. He tells his son that the guards are explaining the rules of the 'game' and that they can eventually win enough points to victoriously ride a tank out of the camp.

As a viewer, the joyful humour of the first half of the movie is replaced with tearful laughter in the second half. It is beautiful and heart-wrenching viewing, as it highlights the powerful combination of hope, humanity and imagination. Even in dire conditions, your mind can create an alternative narrative to positively influence your personal experience of those conditions.

In real life, Viktor Frankl, a Holocaust survivor, neurologist, psychiatrist and developer of logotherapy (the idea that humans are most motivated by a search for meaning), accredited Stoicism as a spiritual survival mechanism during his time in a concentration camp. In the book *Man's Search for Meaning*, Frankl wrote a memoir of his spiritual survivorship:

> 'In spite of all the enforced physical and mental primitiveness of the life in a concentration camp, it was possible for spiritual life to deepen. Sensitive people who were used to a rich intellectual life may have suffered much pain (they were often of a delicate constitution), but the damage to their inner selves was less. They were able to retreat from their terrible surroundings to a life of inner riches and spiritual freedom. Only in this way can one explain the apparent paradox that some prisoners of a less hardy makeup often seemed to survive camp life better than did those of a robust nature.'

Organisational change can be brutal. At times, the workplace can feel energetically heavy – like a storm cloud sitting above the glass, revolving door as you walk into the building each day. Often, that is because the survival of the business is riding on its ability to change. It becomes an 'adapt or die' situation. Business transformation is an imperative. For imagination, ideation and innovation to have any chance of surfacing in such heavy conditions, there needs to be an environment of hope, optimism and creativity, which will nurture growth. This final chapter is dedicated to guiding you back from burnout to brilliance by reigniting your imagination and creativity.

IGNITE YOUR CREATIVE VALUE

Think of your creative value as the way in which you uniquely contribute to your work, your team and your legacy. In the past, when you were drained of energy and spiralling down, it became obvious that your creativity, focus and optimism also flowed down the drain at a rapid pace. Initially, your mind was filled with shame about the absence of a past talent that you were once recognised for, but later this shame was replaced with apathy and you mentally checked out.

But if you want to recover from burnout and *Reimagine Change*, you must welcome back creativity in your life. Creativity enriches every facet of life. Creativity equips you to continuously transform. Creativity trumps technical qualities every day of the week.

A LinkedIn Learning article, titled 'The Skills Companies Need Most in 2020 – and How to Learn Them', found: *'Topping this year's list are creativity, collaboration, persuasion, and emotional intelligence – all skills that demonstrate how we work with others and bring new ideas to the table.'* Despite what you may think, creativity is a learned behaviour – not an inherent trait. In other words, anyone can learn to become more creative, or ignite their creative value, providing they know how. We'll discuss this in more detail soon.

At this point in the book, having worked through all of the previous chapters, any residual emotional numbness should have been replaced with a stronger sense of safety, self-worth and emotional presence. At about this point of the journey, your compass starts to flicker as your mental and emotional energy strengthens. So, where should you direct this newfound energy?

Two options present themselves here. You may be thinking either of returning to work or perhaps pivoting in your career. Now that you have evolved, the idea of 'going back' to your old job, your old life, your old behaviours can seem quite confronting. Why? Because something is niggling away at you. You may have an underlying sense that you may not get your creative mojo back. Am I right?

Don't worry – I am not going to allow you to stand rooted in rationalisation. The answer once again lies within. Imagination and creativity can be used as an anchor to help you climb out of burnout, or as a bridge to reintegrate you back into daily life. It also has the added bonus of positioning you to thrive in tumultuous times as well as opening the door to more social connection, too.

The VIA Institute of Character shared this insight about the character strength of creativity:

> *'There are two essential components to creativity – originality and adaptiveness. A creative individual generates ideas or behaviours that are novel or unusual and these make a positive contribution to the individual's life or the lives of others.'* *According to the institute, someone who identifies as creative would say to themselves, 'I am creative, conceptualising something useful, coming up with ideas that result in something worthwhile.'*

CAPTAIN'S ORDERS

There is no right or wrong way to explore creativity. At the end of the day, it comes down to what resonates with you. But to give you some context on the topic, here's an overview of six models that define and access creative intelligence in different ways:

- Theory of multiple intelligences (psychology)
- Triarchic theory of intelligence (psychology)
- Investment theory of creativity (psychology)
- Disney Method (neuro-linguistic programming)
- Flow state (psychology)
- Creative intelligence (neuroscience and anthropology)

I. THEORY OF MULTIPLE INTELLIGENCES

In 1983, Harvard psychologist Howard Gardner presented the theory of multiple intelligences in the book *Frames of Mind: The Theory of Multiple Intelligences*. While individuals will show a strength or heightened skew towards one of the following intelligences, they usually embody more than one. For example, many sport stars also excel in interpersonal skills and go on to become team managers in non-sport-related fields.

Visual-spatial intelligence

You are able to use your 'mind's eye' to visually see patterns and practise spatial judgement. In other words, how things move and their relation to each other. This allows you to excel at puzzles, graphs, building designs and visual arts.

Linguistic-verbal intelligence

You have a way with words, either verbally or through writing. Extending on ideas or conversing in a succinct manner is one of your talents. This positions you as a natural storyteller or debater.

Logical-mathematical intelligence

You are the numbers guy or girl. Your natural flair sees you loving logic, recognising patterns, problem solving and absorbed in analytics. Great mathematicians, scientists and programmers also possess this strength.

Bodily-kinaesthetic intelligence

You have 'moves like Jagger' or, more specifically, body movement comes naturally to you. Whether this is the methodical motion of brick laying or skills in sports and/or dancing, you are known for your exceptional hand-eye coordination.

Musical intelligence

You have a sensitivity to the rhythm, pitch, tone and melody of music. This allow you to excel at music-related endeavours such as singing, playing instruments, composing music and performing in general.

Interpersonal intelligence

You are a 'people person', known for developing strong relationships. This sees you skilled at both verbal and non-verbal communication. You recognise when group dynamics are shifting and are proactive at resolving problems.

Intrapersonal intelligence

You are a 'deep thinker' concerned with human states and emotions. You love to spend time in observation of your own self and others. Daydreaming allows you to be fluid in your creativity and this often converts to writing or social sciences.

Naturalistic intelligence

You are at your best when you are 'one with nature', whether this is travelling and exploring or simply appreciating the natural world in your own back garden. Your respect for Mother Nature sees you flourish in the context of food, farming, nature and biology.

Key insights

There are two key points to remember here. The first is to know and articulate your primary and secondary intelligence types with your team and family. This will allow you to understand the creative mix within the group and explore how you can seek out more diversity of thought. The second key point is: Don't limit yourself to focusing on just one or two intelligence types. While organisations are focused on you 'playing to your strengths', why not explore and be curious about how developing secondary intelligences might enhance your human 'wholeness'?

2. TRIARCHIC THEORY OF INTELLIGENCE

In 1988, Robert Sternberg, a psychologist, psychometrician and former president of the American Psychology Association, developed a three-part theory, known as the triarchic theory of intelligence. The three meta-components of the theory are:

Practical intelligence
The ability to read and adapt to the demands of the environment. This includes the terms 'street smarts' and 'common sense'.

Analytical intelligence
The ability to analyse, evaluate and problem solve using mental steps and processes. This includes academic application of theories and formulas.

Creative intelligence
The ability to extend an idea beyond the supposed given. To draw on experiences, insight and imagination to generate new ideas from different perspectives.

The combination of these three intelligences comprises successful intelligence:

Successful intelligence
This is the balanced integration of the three meta-components to attain *success* in life's social context, noting that success is subjective to the individual.

Key insights
There are two key points to remember here. The first is to invite curiosity by using your voice and encouraging others to question

assumptions. Rather than follow organisational groupthink, think creatively and schedule in time to do so. Encourage inquiry-based conversations to harness the collective intelligence of the group. The second key point is that risk-taking is encouraged. Stop playing it safe and start pushing the boundaries of possibility. Seek out support from those who have pioneered risk-taking, creative endeavours or innovative solutions. Seek to learn how they turned ideas into prototypes.

3. INVESTMENT THEORY OF CREATIVITY

In 1991, the same psychologist, Robert Sternberg, presented the investment theory of creativity. This theory states, *'Creativity is a decision in the same way investing is. People are not born creative or uncreative. Rather, they develop a set of attitudes toward life that characterise those who are willing to go their own way.'* The attitudes and aspects of this theory are:

Attitudes of creativity
A willingness to redefine problems, take sensible risks, 'sell' ideas others may not see value in (classic start-up mindset), persevere through obstacles and examine one's own preconceptions to expand the limitations of creativity.

Aspects of creativity
Abilities, knowledge, styles of thinking, personality attributes, motivation, intrinsic motivation and environment.

Key insights
There are two key points to remember here. The first is that attitudes are teachable. The key to learning these attitudes is unlearning the old ones. For example, compliance-focused

organisations are entrenched in 'doing the right thing' and, therefore, are typically more risk-averse when it comes to unearthing their creativity. The second key point is that reskilling trumps renovations. Organisations that are eager to get your creativity flowing tend to do you a disservice by focusing on the external attributes (for example, office renovations) at the expense of investing in your upskilling and motivation.

4. DISNEY METHOD

In 1994, neuro-linguistic programmer Robert Dilts, in consultation with none other than Walt Disney himself, modelled what came to be known as the Disney method. The purpose of this strategy was to assist in character development by 'switching' mental attitudes. Some prefer to stand and do this exercise, literally moving into a different position one at a time, around the 'four square of roles' to assume each of the archetypes. The four elements of the Disney method are:

The outsider

You begin by assuming an analytical role as you assess the character, client or problem at hand, with an external or macro view of what is taking place. It is very matter of fact and data driven, subject to availability. State the facts at hand and then move on.

The dreamer

You transition into a carefree, easy-going state and let the ideas flow out of your mind. No filters, no holding back and no judgement. Only free-flow ideas, both big and small, being captured on paper. The key is to get them written out.

The realist

You transition into the now and assess the current state of accessible resources (time/money/people power) to turn your ideas into a reality. It is less critical in tone, and more practical and open-minded about what could be possible.

The critic

You transition into the critic. As implied, you get down into the detail, leave no stone unturned, and assess risks, red lights and flaws, taking your time to carefully map this out for further reflection by yourself and others.

Key insights

There are two key points to remember here. The first is: Don't judge; do. Don't be anxious about this exercise – it's fun and easy to get started. If standing and using your body as an extension of your brain feels foreign, then mark out a four-square quadrant on your whiteboard, notepad or journal. Remember that Walt Disney used this method to make in excess of 170 movies, so what are you waiting for?! The second key point is that, if the Disney method resonates with you, you may consider exploring the method outlined in Dr. Edward de Bono's *Six Thinking Hats* as an alternative for idea and perspective generation. These types of methods are designed to give you permission to think, feel and experience another person or archetype other than your habitual self. For example, how might assuming the role of an upstart entrepreneur or the head of a global corporation like Apple, Uber or Thrive Global shift your perspective and ignite your imagination?

5. FLOW STATE

In 2008, legendary psychologist Mihaly Csikszentmihalyi published the book *Flow: The Psychology of Optimal Experience*. He states, '*A person can make himself happy or miserable, regardless of what is actually happening outside, just by changing the contents of consciousness.*'

With regard to flow, he shares, '*I developed a theory of optimal experience based on the concept of flow – the state in which people are so involved in an activity that nothing else seems to matter; the experience itself is so enjoyable that people will do it even at great cost, for the sheer sake of doing it.*' Flow is when you feel your best *and* perform your best. It is time to forget the modern obsession with productivity and focus on feeling your best to coax out your brilliance.

In a TEDx Talk titled 'Hacking the Flow State to Accelerate Human Evolution', founder of the Flow Genome Project, Jamie Wheal, describes flow as 'being in the pocket' (think jazz musicians), a 'runner's high' (think athletes) and being 'in the zone' (think high-performance individuals). Wheal gives these examples of what happens in flow:

The 'what' of flow
- You drop into a theta state and wait for gamma state (from subconscious to peak focus).
- You experience a loss of self-awareness; you lose track of time and nothing else matters.
- Your neo-cortex or executive brain goes offline, as does your ego.
- Your nervous system resets as your stress hormones escape.
- You optimise your biological and neurological self-system.
- You come alive with an ease of creative thought on the flow spectrum.

The 'how' of flow

Steven Kotler, Wheal's business partner and author of *The Rise of Superman*, shares a four-step approach to induce flow. Here's an overview:

Struggle

You transition to a semi-agitated, unsustainable beta state. (If you need a refresher on the different brain waves, including beta waves, revisit the section on theta hacking in Chapter 5.)

Stretch your capability and learning into your peak zone with work, sports or hobbies that you are passionate and purposeful about. This stretch should be verging on 'unsustainable struggle'. Remember to practise self-compassion when your self-critic enters the scene.

Release

You transition to a slower alpha state.

Stop what you are doing. Sever your thoughts by going for a walk or taking a physical break away from your work. This is when the brain magic happens. Kotler states, *'Mental release results in the release of nitric oxide release which allow dopamine (reward systems) and endorphins to flood our brain and allow us to access flow state.'*

Flow

You enter the theta state (where your subconscious resides) and on occasion transition into the gamma state.

Flow deactivates the prefrontal cortex (where your inner critic resides). It is not forced. Rather, you allow it to happen. Three additional enhancers for flow activation include: a) social risk, such as giving your word or publicly announcing you are striving to achieve a certain outcome, b) working in a novel space, and c) seeking faster feedback from others to drive corrective action.

Recover
You transition back to delta brain waves, responsible for memory consolidation.

Here, your proactive mind requires adequate dopamine and serotonin to be at the ready in your system to draw up, while your regenerative mind then seeks ways to replenish the post-flow hangover in your brain. Again, sleep is the key – and plenty of it! Go and sleep it off.

So, if you have been conditioned to believe that productivity is king, consider that perhaps it is better to access flow in the first instance. Kotler's book refers to research by McKinsey & Company, which found *executives that produced flow state saw a 500% increase in productivity afterwards.*

Key insights
There are two key points to remember here. The first is that flow is a state. The term 'state' confirms that flow is not fixed or permanent. Rather, it comes and goes, as depicted by the four-stage cycle just outlined. During this time, a mix of five performance-enhancing neurochemicals (norepinephrine, dopamine, serotonin, anandamide and endorphins) occur in the brain simultaneously. Once you *respect* the four-stage cycle, you will easily follow the process in a way that best suits your personal experience.

The second key point is to give yourself space. Don't obsess over reaching this as a short-term goal or milestone. Much like learning cooking, yoga or meditation, there is a process and a duress that must be honoured. Pro tip: Make time to *take* time away from intensive work and regenerate.

6. CREATIVE INTELLIGENCE

In 2013, Bruce Nussbaum, innovation expert and anthropology enthusiast, released the book *Creative Intelligence* to help readers navigate the unknown. The book explores how you would measure creative intelligence (CQ) in the measure that you would standardise maths, verbal skills and writing. He advocates for methods beyond typical memorisation and individual genius. The five elements of creative intelligence are:

Knowledge mining
You deeply value knowing your audience and their needs intimately. Think about the entrepreneurial mindset. Successful entrepreneurs approach the same age-old problems as everyone else in a new way. The problem they're aiming to solve may have been previously dismissed by others.

Framing
You are able to recognise how you interpret the world or what lens you view situations through. Awareness of framing allows you to 'reframe' over and over again to gain multiple perspectives.

Playing
You enjoy the game of problem solving. You bring renewed energy and enthusiasm to 'playing around' with how things are formed, perceived and done. You are creative in how you flex between ideas.

Making

Your creativity evolves into something tactile, like a prototype through the creative construct of making. The platform Kickstarter is highlighted as an example of socialising capitalism again. Remember, if you can think it, you can make it!

Pivoting

You have the ability to explode your idea into a game changer. Don't sweat the small details, or outsource them and focus on how you become the new or dominant player in a community, an industry or the world.

Key insights

There are two key points to remember, or consider, here. The first is to start a 'magic circle'. Magic circles can eventuate anywhere (work/school/social) and typically involve two to five people who a) trust each other, b) invite an element of play together, and c) connect dots of information together. Examples include rock bands, start-up co-founders who start off as friends, and children playfully working through activities.

The second key point is that creative anxiety is real. It's also incredibly damaging, in that it wastes your time, energy and natural talent. Neuroscientist Joseph LeDoux described anxiety as *'the price we pay for an ability to imagine the future.'*

Consider spending some time learning more about theories of creativity. This will help to spark curiosity and validate the importance of creativity in your mind.

AWAKEN YOUR CREATIVE BRILLIANCE

These days, when young children learn to ride a bike, they usually start by learning on a balance bike or a bike that has training wheels attached to it. This allows them to build up their confidence and competence at an equal rate. Well, the same can be said about creativity.

Right now, organisations are demanding that employees – and especially leaders – become overnight innovators. For many non-specialists, this feels like a daunting task. At a macro level, it helps to understand that organisational innovation requires a combination of strategy, structure, culture and capabilities to create value offerings. At a micro level, the onus is on you to reset your mindset and accelerate.

There are six mindset magnifiers to fast-track creative confidence. Three relate to identity (who you need to be) and three relate to ideation (what will guide you).

IDENTITY
1. Belief
2. Energy
3. Intention

IDEATION
1. Imagination
2. Creative thinking
3. Design thinking

Please note that concepts such as diversity, inclusion and storytelling are highly relevant to the co-creative process, whereby you spark creativity in collaboration with others. However, as we're focusing on the *individual* mindset to fast-track creative confidence, only these six sub-topics will be explored. Let's explore each one now.

IDENTITY

By starting with your identity, change will feel effortless when it stems from a secure mindset. Here, a quote from Michelangelo, the renaissance sculpturist, artist and painter, best explains what an identity of innate creativity feels like: *'The sculpture is already complete within the marble block, before I start my work. It is already there; I just have to chisel away the superfluous material.'* With that in mind, let's now look at the first mindset magnifier, belief.

I. BELIEF

Often, you can be your own worst enemy by hiding behind excuses and self-imposed limitations. To reinstate self-belief, start by listing out your inner critic limitations. Let's look at four common limitations now.

Limitation #1: 'I don't have the title or qualifications to do that type of work.'
Don't mistake assumptions for hard facts. You do not have to be a designated creative in order to be creative. You do not have to be a designated innovator to be innovative. You do not have to be a designated design thinker to ideate. You *do* have to be accountable for shifting your mindset. Think like the leader you are and back yourself.

As life coach and motivational speaker Marie Forleo says, everything is 'figureoutable', so say yes and your mind will get to work, working it out for you. Meanwhile, Mel Robbins (also a motivational speaker) shares her science-backed five-second rule, whereby you count down from five to one in your mind (five-four-three-two-one). This then activates your prefrontal cortex, prompting you to take immediate action in a positive and productive direction. So, no more excuses.

Limitation #2: 'I don't have the materials.'

Don't let your materials define your ability to start. Cavemen painted on cave walls and children write on the sand to express their creativity. As an adult, you have access to more materials than you could possibly imagine. In this tech-obsessed world, you can find amazing inspiration by searching for templates and playbooks on the internet or using one of the latest apps on your mobile.

However, going old school with a pencil and a single sheet of paper can also be a fantastic way to get the creative juices flowing. Don't forget that many a good idea has started on the back of a bar coaster or napkin, too! Your success hinges on your ability to give yourself permission for your ideas to flow out. That is where the magic lies.

Limitation #3: 'I am not that way inclined – I never have been.'

Don't let preconceived ideas of nature versus nurture hold you back. When you were a child, you may have been told that you weren't as creative as the other children. Or you may have given up by default – work and life have gotten ridiculously busy. Right?!

Allowing your creativity to lie dormant is a common tale, but that doesn't mean it's irreversible. Look around you. Everything that you surround yourself with represents creativity. The clothes you wear, the books you read, the company you keep. All of these weave new colours and new perspectives into your life. If your rainbow is dull, make the effort to switch out what de-energises you and replace it with what does energise you.

Limitation #4: 'I'd rather not put my ideas out there. What if people laugh at me?'
Don't be the person responsible for dimming your own light. When I hear this phrase, it usually signifies a few red flags. Either you are not engaged in interesting, impactful work, or, if you are, you either doubt your capabilities or your self-worth, or you work in an environment where psychological safety is absent.

Only once your inner critic has been silenced, or at least muffled, will a new attitude be supported by your belief system. At this stage, consider adopting what is affectionately known as 'an attitude of gratitude' to your creative work. When you shift from 'I have to be creative' to 'I want to be creative' to 'I get to be creative', you leverage the power of gratitude and feel-good neurochemicals to kick-start the creative process. Please go back and read those three phrases again, pausing between each to see if you notice a difference in the way they make you feel. Remember that so few people in the world get to put their creativity to use day in and day out. It is a privilege to cherish rather than waste.

2. ENERGY

In his book *The Element*, world-renowned education and creativity expert Sir Ken Robinson shares that passion and fulfilment are, for the most part, absent in our community. According to Robinson, '*Most adults have no ideas of their true talents or what they are capable of... Human resources, like natural resources, are often buried deep. You have to go looking for it.'*

Robinson also states, *'People do their best when they do something they love. When they are in their element. When you are in your element, you are doing something that you have a natural feel for or a natural aptitude.'* Another way to describe being in your element is being in the zone or being in a flow state. The reality of flow is that it is not always achievable immediately. For some people, it is a large leap on the ladder of inference (or how you learn). A simple, gentler way to get started is by engaging in creative activities.

Pursuing creative activities

The time is now to replace 'good for you' activities with joyful or creative activities. In neuro-linguistic programming (NLP), they teach the VAKOG (visual, auditory, kinaesthetic, olfactory, gustatory) representation system as a way of recognising how each person experiences the world through a different sensory lens. Here's a brief outline:

- **Visual:** Your preference is to experience the world through imagery and pictures.
- **Auditory:** Your preference is to experience the world through listening, talking, sounds and music.
- **Kinaesthetic:** Your preference is to experience the world through touch, role-modelling and in-person experiences that 'feel right'.
- **Olfactory:** Your preference is to experience the world by leading with your nose through smell and scent.
- **Gustatory:** Your preference is to experience the world by tasting your way through life.

198 | REIMAGINE CHANGE

By recognising which is your preferred or dominant representation system, you can more easily align to creative activities that will spark more enjoyment. Here's a beginner's list for each one. Obviously, there are many more you can add yourself.

VISUAL CREATIVITY	AUDITORY CREATIVITY	KINAESTHETIC CREATIVITY	OLFACTORY/ GUSTATORY CREATIVITY
Drawing/ colouring	Singing	Meditating	Cooking
Journaling/ writing	Composing music	Soaking in a bath	Baking
Reading	Creating playlists	Crafting pottery	Perfume making
Photography	Teaching	Sewing/knitting	Wine tasting
Daydreaming	Sound walking	Gifting	Taste testing
Ideating	Listening to audiobooks/ podcasts	Playing games with your children	Chewing gum

3. INTENTION

Regardless of your spirituality, Deepak Chopra is the man in the know when it comes to setting your intention. He states:

'Intention is the starting point of every dream. It is the creative power that fulfils all of our needs, whether for money, relationships, spiritual awakening, or love. An intention is a directed impulse of consciousness that contains the seed form of that which you aim to create. Like real seeds, intentions

can't grow if you hold on to them. Only when you release your intentions into the fertile depths of your consciousness can they grow and flourish.'

Chopra suggests the following practice.

Set the intention: Slip into the silence behind the ego mind, which is accessible via meditation. Release any objectives and desires within yourself, and then stop thinking about them. Remain centred in a state of restful awareness, not allowing doubts or criticism to reduce your optimism. Detach from the outcome by seeking a sense of ease that everything will work out as it should. Let the universe handle the details. In other words, resist the need for control (this takes practice!).

The key question to ask yourself is: How will my intention better influence a positive outcome for all involved? This practice is about raising your emotional energy – something you are in total control of. It's designed to have a very powerful domino effect on all the steps that follow. To further develop your intention, you need to:

- Be empty
- Be mindful
- Be tech-free

Let's explore each of those ideas.

Be empty

The next tip is to 'start with nothing'. Why? Well, as the saying goes, something always comes from nothing. Sounds easy, right? Well, with practice and process, it is. If you have worked through the steps as outlined by Deepak Chopra, your baseline will be stabilised. From this state, you will be ready to empty your monkey mind.

To have a monkey mind is to be consumed with distractions, ideas and to-do lists. It consumes your mental energy as it hinders your ability to switch off the mind and be calm. To move into a more start-ready position, next, you'll need to do a mental download using a jug metaphor.

Empty the jug: Visualise a jug full to the brim with your thoughts and emotions. Now, imagine you are pouring it out. Every last drop. There – that feels better, doesn't it? Enjoy the moment and allow a smile to spread across your face. Next, grab your journal or a piece of paper and write down three to five things you intend to follow up later in the day. This will stop your mind fretting and allow you to be open to receiving new ideas.

When you declutter your mind, your emotions are less likely to be triggered. This jug exercise is brilliant to do before a big meeting, before bed, and any time you need a five-minute break from whatever you're doing. The more you allow your thoughts to flow out, the more space you will have to continually create.

Be mindful

Perhaps you have already developed a routine or practice that you use in times like this. If that is working, then stick with it. Your brain will be soothed by the familiarity. If you don't have a mindful practice, you need one. Remember that when the amygdala sounds the alarm, your executive brain retreats. So, keep trying different practices until your body responds in a way that signals 'this is the one for me'.

Guided meditation and binaural beat therapy are great options if you have headphones nearby. For those new to binaural beats, available on Spotify or YouTube, this is where two different sound frequencies or tones are delivered to the left and right ear. The brain then hears a third tone, which is the mathematical difference of the two tones. Binaural beats are most popular for anxiety, stress and focus. Other popular mindfulness practices include:

Start and end point: Seated in a chair, get a sense of your starting stress level. Rank it between zero and five, with five being the highest. Alternatively, you may want to take your pulse at the beginning and end of any meeting or meditation to compare the difference.

Body scan: Sitting in a chair, take a deep, 'letting go' breath. Now, starting at the top of your head, visualise each part of your body. As you say the body part, give yourself permission to release any tension being held in that area. Methodically work your way down and around your body until you eventually arrive at your feet, at which point you will wiggle your toes to release all residual energy. Next, tell yourself that, right now, you are refreshed and ready for whatever is to come your way.

Mountain meditation: This starts in a similar fashion to the body scan. Once you have taken a 'letting go' breath, picture yourself in any natural setting that is just right for you. I have given the example of a mountain, but it may be a beach, a farm or woodlands. Imagine that you are in the setting and looking around at all the wondrous details. Notice the crunching of the leaves beneath your feet, the sound of the babbling brook nearby, and how you can easily walk through nature to explore more and more details.

After three minutes (you can set a timer if you think that will help), thank Mother Nature for sharing her gifts and begin to return to the consciousness of the seat you are sitting in.

Be tech-free

In *The Neuroscience of Mindfulness*, neuroscientist Stan Rodski shares that '*you don't have to understand any of the in-depth science for mindfulness to work... if the scientific details scare you, then skip the technical parts.*' I love this because, in the era of cognitive overload, sometimes, in a moment of need, you simply need to know 'how' rather than 'why'.

One of the most visible ways to show you are ready and willing to connect with the purpose of creating is to put down your devices (mobile phone, laptop, iPad and so on). If you're in a group setting, call this out and ask everyone to be on the same page or same whiteboard, and not across several different screens.

Your eyes are the windows to the soul and, subconsciously, you are always scanning people around you to confirm whether they are non-threatening, trustworthy and likeable. This is the neuroception, as discussion in Chapter 4. Technology kills this energy instantly. Either be busy being busy or be creative being tech-free.

Next, you need to recognise that attempting to multitask is not only a distraction but a delusion. Mental overload, and switching tasks like air traffic control, slows down productivity and inhibits creativity. In *The Organised Mind*, neuroscientist Daniel Levitin shares why we can't stop ourselves from multitasking, even though we know we should:

'You'd think people would realise they're bad at multitasking and would quit. But a cognitive illusion sets in, fuelled in part by a dopamine-adrenaline feedback loop, in which multitaskers think they are doing great.'

He goes on to suggest that there is an antidote to all this mindlessness:

'The brain has an attentional mode called the "mind wandering mode" [the default mode network] that was only recently identified. This is when thoughts move seamlessly from one to another, often to unrelated thoughts, without you controlling where they go. This brain state acts as a neural reset button, allowing us to come back to our work with a refreshed perspective. Different people find they enter this mode in different ways: reading, a walk in nature, looking at art, meditating, and napping. A fifteen-minute nap can produce the equivalent of a ten-point boost in IQ.'

In short, put your phone away and allow your mind to wander or even shut down for a little while.

IDEATION

Now that we've discussed the three mindset magnifiers related to identity (*who you need to be* in order to fast-track creative confidence), let's explore the three mindset magnifiers related to ideation (*what will guide you* to fast-track it).

4. IMAGINATION

Have you ever closed your eyes only to imagine nothing? You are not alone, especially when overwhelm and exhaustion are contributing factors. Much like guided meditation, guided imagination exercises are also at your fingertips if you need a nudge in the right direction. Let's start with the lemon imagery exercise if you have never done it before.

Lemon exercise: Take a few nice, deep, 'letting go' breaths and notice how your body responds as you begin to focus on your breath. Using your imagination, I'd like you to picture yourself in a kitchen that is very familiar to you. Either your own kitchen or someone else's. This may even be the kitchen from your childhood – the one that is associated with positive memories. Whichever kitchen you settle upon, make sure it has positive associations.

Imagine now that you are standing at the doorway leading into the kitchen. Before you are the usual items you'd expect to see in a kitchen. A fridge, a sink, a stovetop. Notice the family kitchen table next and focus in on the chair you usually sit in. Next, you notice that there is a lovely aroma coming out of the oven; someone has been baking. Whatever it is smells delicious, like your favourite baked treats. Next to the oven is a toaster and stacked behind the toaster is a selection of wooden chopping boards. Choose one and slide it out, placing it all the way down onto the counter. The knife block is in reaching distance and you reach over and wrap your hand around the big knife. Sliding it carefully out, you place it on the same chopping board.

To your left is a bowl of fruit and sitting on the top is a shiny, vibrant, yellow lemon. Its glossiness is spectacular. You reach for it and notice the hard, waxy feeling in your hand. Raising it up to your nose, you sniff it and the lemony scent floods your nostrils. Placing it on the chopping board, you now pick up the big knife and you slice into the middle of the lemon, cutting it in half. With two halves lying before you, you admire the uniform pattern of the jewel-like pulp. You notice that a few drops of juice have run onto the board. After putting the knife down, with that same hand you reach and pick up one half of the lemon. As you bring it closer to your mouth, the wonderful lemony scent is much stronger now. With the lemon right before your lips, you close your eyes and open your mouth and bite into the lemon.

Now, if you were invested in reading along and using your imagination, all of your sensors should have awakened. Perhaps your mouth even started to water! When this exercise is done in a group setting, participants usually look around to see who has a sour face afterwards. There is a very high likelihood that even though no lemon existed, in the theatre of your mind, the imagery was so powerful that by the time you bit into the lemon, you screwed up your face in response to the imagined bitterness.

In *Make Health Happen*, San Francisco State University lecturer Erik Pepper refers to a study of 131 college students. After completing the lemon imagery exercise, ninety-four per cent of the students reported an increase in salivation, which is a parasympathetic nervous system response. This highlights the fact that thoughts and mental imagery can be powerful change agents for your physiology. This relates to the placebo (positive) and nocebo (negative) effects when a person consumes sugar pills, thinking they are medicine with certain side effects. What the person hears (in this case, from the doctor or nurse) then influences their own inner narrative, and this aids their mind to mentally forecast and fulfil their future. Pro tip: Leverage, rather than dismiss, the power of your mindset and imagination activation, especially when visualising positive mental imagery.

5. CREATIVE THINKING

Your mind is full of ideas – some are average and some are exceptional. All ideas have the potential to expand and create immense value if you create the conditions for them to flourish. You simply have to choose the optimal moments to unleash them. In the TED Talk 'Creative thinking – how to get out of the box and generate ideas', Giovanni Corazza, a university professor of science and the application of creative thinking, states, *'To think creatively, to go out of the box, is not a luxury. It's a necessity for us, and for our dignity as human beings.'*

He goes on to describe the 'ingredients for creative thinking':

- **Awareness of 'the box'.** This refers to the restrictions and restraints of your brain. This includes your genetic heritage, your environment, your indirect experiences (school or university) and your direct experiences (successes or failures).

- **Awareness of 'outside the box'.** This is divergent information that is seemingly not relevant but can cross the borders of your mind and take you far into expanded thinking, or what Corazza calls 'valuing long thinking'. Here, the combined divergent thinking (generation of many ideas or brainstorming) and convergent thinking (generation of a singular, 'right' solution) becomes lateral thinking (generation of outside-of-the-box thinking) because you are using both sides.

- **Awareness of many possible alternatives.** This is the removal or letting go of your need to be right by looking for many alternatives and not correct answers alone. Perfectionists, authoritarians and specialists will relate to this one.

- **Awareness of self-limitations.** This is your temptation to reject or kill your own ideas. This is when self-doubt fogs creative freedom with the mindset of 'if this is correct, somebody else would have done it before me'.

For example, in change leadership workshops, the 'Destination Postcard' exercise is a simple, yet powerful, individual divergent thinking exercise. Here, workshop participants are asked to imagine what short-term and long-term changes to the business they would implement if they were the leader of the business (with access to unlimited resources). This is an effective way to give individuals the freedom to imagine and express their unique perspectives before comparing and contrasting with the group.

6. DESIGN THINKING

Methods come in and out of fashion faster than you can update your LinkedIn profile. What is industry buzz one day can quickly become industry bullsh*t the next. Design thinking, on the other hand, has been around for fifty years. It's tried and tested, and has stood the test of time. Yet, so many non-experts shy away from it, preferring to leave all the glory to the experts. Don't let that discourage you. Invest time in learning more extensively about design thinking, and about the art and science of learning in general.

Design thinking is steeped in both method and mindset. The internet will provide you with the methodology specifics. Here, our focus will be on the mindset aspect or the primer phase, which will get you in the right headspace. All the rest can be learned on the go, once you have the necessary mindset.

So, how might we apply key elements of the design thinking mindset to awaken your creative brilliance at work and beyond?

There are four core ways to connect to a design thinking mindset:

- Connect with just one other (empathy)
- Connect with existing wisdom (experience)
- Connect with your inner child (playfulness)
- Connect with celebration (pure joy)

Connect with just one other

You've got this. Innately, you are an expert at connecting with other tribe members. Think about it. In your life, you have an inner circle of friends with whom you have forged strong relationships. Trust is a given. As such, if one of your inner-circle friends seeks out your guidance or expertise on something they are grappling with, you will generally find it comes very naturally to you to support them through to a better outcome than where they are at. Why? Because you intimately know and empathise with this friend.

In design thinking, the same principles apply. At the heart of every problem is a sentient, human being experiencing or being impacted by one core problem. Use your new learnings about self-compassion and compassion for others to genuinely empathise with them. All design thinking anchors off this human-centric principle. Remind your brain this is easy and comes naturally to you.

Only when you are mindfully present can you attempt to really step into the mind of another individual. Zone in on a single human being or persona that best represents someone experiencing the problem at hand. Once you know who that is and what their pain points are, the best advice is to embody *their* needs as *your* needs. This is often referred to as 'walking in their shoes', 'sitting in the trenches together', or commencing role play as if you were them.

When you are in service of others, when you genuinely want to help just one person solve what they are grappling with, you recognise and respect the common humanity aspect at hand. At its core, this is one human being holding a candle for another human being. Simply recognising and responding to their darkness. This is your opportunity to be generous. To draw on your heart, your wisdom and your unique life experience to solve their problem. This human-centric mindset is the gift that will give time and time again in your career, your work and your life.

Connect with existing wisdom

Rather than piling on the pressure to do more and learn more, how might the idea of simply being enough give you the strength to forge ahead in confidence, right here, right now?

The secret is to think, feel and believe that you and those around you are human gold mines. Lying just beneath the surface is years of collective experience, insight and wisdom that can be drawn from and connected to the problem at hand when an environment of psychological safety, courage and fearlessness is present.

In an article by *Wired*, the late Steve Jobs had this to say about design and creativity:

> 'Creativity is just connecting things. When you ask creative people how they did something, they feel a little guilty because they didn't really do it, they just saw something. It seemed obvious to them after a while. That's because they were able to connect experiences they've had and synthesise new things. And the reason they were able to do that was that they've had more experiences or they have thought more about their experiences than other people.'

Become versed in articulating your strengths, your interests and your adversities. Know what lights you up and what you've learned from, and draw from those experiences. These can be drawn from different decades, different industries and different perspectives. Leverage the wisdom that already lies within and connect it to the very work you are doing day in and day out. This means you are not exerting energy on learning the new, but rather recognising and repurposing the learnings that lie within. Remember that no connection or idea is a 'bad one'. Each one inches you closer to an outcome, through a series of test and learn iterations and feedback loops.

Connect with your inner child

Before you jump to conclusions, let me put your mind at ease. This is not about consoling the wounded child of your youth. In the context of creativity, you are invited to reconnect with your inner child because this represents fearless curiosity, endless energy reserves and a joy in simply figuring something out. Children are an absolute delight to watch in their unbridled 'I've worked it out' a-ha moments.

The collaboration experts will have you believe that co-creation is about trust, diversity and inclusion, and value creation. This type of corporate language shuts down the very asset that lights up teams and individuals of all ages. That asset is play. When you invite playfulness into any environment, sparks fly. Humans love being given the opportunity to let loose, to laugh and to reveal the lighter side of themselves. The secret to playfulness is knowing that it is subjective and, therefore, needs to be audience appropriate. For example, this may simply be the joy of the challenge rather than the proverbial bucket of Lego in the boardroom. At the core of all business and personal transformations is relationships. Relationships are about respecting not only your journey but the journeys of those around you. When in doubt, prioritise connection and relationships, both the old and the new.

In a 2006 TED Talk, Peter Skillman discussed the famous 'Marshmallow Challenge', designed to encourage team collaboration. The challenge played out like this: a room full of people – representing four very different demographics – was divided up into teams of four. Each team was given twenty sticks of spaghetti, one yard of tape, one yard of string and one marshmallow. Using only those items, and with a time limit of just eighteen minutes, teams were challenged to build the tallest free-standing structure possible, with the marshmallow on the top.

Of the different teams Skillman had assembled, ranging from CEOs to business school students to children, it was the kindergarten children who achieved the best results. The secret to their success? They just kept at it. They focused all their attention on testing and retesting, learning from each other's mistakes, and challenging the rules until it was time to stop. They didn't allow any power struggles or critical mind theorising to impact the clock or the outcome.

Consider how being fearless, and inviting others to be fearless, too (by channelling your child-like curiosity, mindful absorption and free-spirited playfulness), could optimise the change agenda.

Connect with celebration

Striving towards big, hairy, audacious goal (BHAG) attainment blocks you from the joy of incremental progress. Chunk down the milestones, loosen up the expectations that you hold yourself to, and celebrate the here and now. Today is a reason to celebrate because tomorrow may never come. In tough times, this feels unrealistic. Do it anyway. Throw caution to the wind and do your happy dance or whatever micro-moment brings you joy. Train your brain to celebrate daily progress rather than distant outcomes.

Internally, allow a sense of pride to bubble up. Allow yourself to smile at how far you have come, regardless of how far you have to go. If your workplace doesn't believe or allow for joy or human emotion, don't let this deter you from recognising and assigning meaning to your own work and the work that your team members are contributing to. When you top up your energetic vibration, it ripples out to others. In a sea of corporate black, be the warm sunshine. Allow yourself to glow and invite others to do the same, especially if it is not 'the done thing'!

Congratulate yourself on following through and getting this far. Remember that decisive action is the antithesis to feeling stuck and overwhelmed. Too often, people feel that their efforts, ideas and time are unappreciated or not valued. Human beings love to feel that their creativity and contribution matter. Respect them, praise them and thank them. Be more human than every other manager or leader out there. It takes very little effort but can be incredibly fulfilling for all involved. Be *that* leader.

In a *Fast Company* article titled 'How To Tap Into The Neuroscience of Winning', Mark Lukens states, '*The neuroscience of success can be used to motivate employees as well as to identify the areas where we're going wrong. For one thing, there can be no feedback loop in the first place if we don't provide employees with those initial feelings of success. Investing in your team members and keeping them engaged for the long haul means offering them early opportunities to achieve things that actually matter, not just delivering hollow praise.*'

So, maybe next time, instead of focusing on stress and struggle, focus on perseverance and possibility. Remember that this is only the tip of the iceberg to ignite the spark within. I encourage you to be courageous in trying new things, learning new processes, and evolving beyond a status quo designed to keep you playing small.

Have a go, because you never know how far it will take you. Start thinking about what could go right and use that as fuel to ignite your creative fire. Inspire yourself to take action and awaken your creative brilliance today. *Don't* leave it to chance. *Don't* default to 'the way things are done'. *Don't* allow your insecurities to limit your potential. *Do* be proactive. *Do* nurture your creativity as well as your career. *Do* give your brilliant, creative mind permission to shine in all facets of your life.

TAP INTO YOUR HUM

Shonda Rhimes is the writer, producer and executive director of multiple hit TV shows including *Grey's Anatomy, Scandal, How to Get Away with Murder* and *The Catch*. In her 2016 TED Talk, titled 'My Year of Saying Yes to Everything', Rhimes shared her journey from writer to executive producer to self-proclaimed titan, responsible for $350 million worth of TV production at the time. She also debunks the myth that being a writer is a dreamy job. On the contrary, it is full of demands, decisions and deadlines. (Something I can attest to!) Rhimes goes on to passionately describe her dedication to her work:

> 'When I'm hard at work, when I'm deep in it, there is no other feeling. For me, my work is at all times building a nation out of thin air. It is manning the troops. It is painting a canvas. It is hitting every high note. It is running a marathon. It is being Beyoncé. And it is all of those things at the same time. I love working. It is creative and mechanical and exhausting and exhilarating and hilarious and disturbing and clinical and maternal and cruel and judicious, and what makes it all so good is the hum. There is some kind of shift inside me when the work gets good. A hum begins in my brain, and it grows and it grows and that hum sounds like the open road, and I could drive it forever.'

Much like the cadence of her TV shows – in which a character or storyline takes a turn for the worse – there is inevitably a 'dip' in the creative process. Rhimes asks:

*'So, what do you do when the thing you do, the work you love,
tastes like dust?... If you have been to the hum and you know
the hum and it stops, who are you? What are you?'*

If you are reading this book, you know this moment. It's the
realisation that the door to creativity, joy and flow has slammed
shut, opening the door to presenteeism, apathy and change fatigue.
So, what can you learn from Rhimes about bouncing forward to
a better version of the hum – something she believes is within
everyone's reach? She states, *'It's about playing in general. Give
yourself fifteen minutes. Find what makes you feel good. Just figure
it out and play in that arena... The very act of not working has made
it possible for the hum to return, as if the hum's engine could only
refuel while I was away... Work doesn't work without play.'*

CHAPTER SUMMARY

That brings us to the end of Chapter 6, the final chapter of *Reimagine Change*. Now is your time to make yourself *hum* again. I encourage you to go forward confidently, with your own innate resources to ignite your imagination, to cultivate your unique creativity, and to unite in co-creative endeavours to solve tomorrow's greatest challenges today. Before I share my final thoughts with you, let's review the key points discussed in Chapter 6:

- Ignite your creative value not only to survive but to thrive in the future of work.

- Broaden your theoretical knowledge of creativity-inducing models, including these six:
  - > Theory of multiple intelligences
  - > Triarchic theory of intelligence
  - > Investment theory of creativity
  - > Disney method
  - > Flow state
  - > Creative intelligence

- Awaken your creative brilliance, leveraging six mindset magnifiers:
  - > Belief
  - > Energy
  - > Intention
  - > Imagination
  - > Creative thinking
  - > Design thinking

- Regardless of your title or tenure, you are capable of making meaningful contributions at work and beyond through your unique voice, creative brilliance and collaborative spirit.

- Passion and purpose have been shown to lead to workaholism and burnout. However, this can be overcome (without having to quit your job) by integrating incremental life and work 'hum' by promoting more moments of play.

CONCLUSION

'The secret of real change is to focus all of your energy,
not on fighting the old, but on building the new.'

– SOCRATES

C ongratulations! Upon completing the final chapter, I hope
you are energised to *Reimagine Change*. This book is based
on my belief that there is an abundance of change capable
individuals with incredible, creative minds waiting to be seen,
heard and appreciated.

The unspoken reality is that no one is immune to the personal
disruption and derailing that can eventuate from living in a world
of fast-paced change expectations. Among all this uncertainty,
what *is* certain is that change is only going to speed up. The negative impact of this will be a rise in chronic stress, change fatigue
and burnout, which will overflow into an already overburdened
mental health system. In this transitional era of test and learn, it
is imperative that more of us talk about our struggles and how
we overcame them.

Before you go, it is important to wrap things up on a more opti-
mistic note. So, let's walk shoulder to shoulder one last time and
reflect on our journey up until now.

FROM KNOW TO GROW

In Part 1, the opening chapters contrasted organisational promises of 'adapt and thrive' with the intrapersonal experience of 'crash and burn'. This was designed to honour you for the complex, perfectly imperfect, sentient being that you are. At the very beginning of the book, you heard the story of Jack spiralling down and out. You also heard my personal experience of peak stretch, along with examples of my personal values and why they matter.

In Part 2, my goal was to arm you with resources to aid your quest to become change capable. These chapters were designed to see you bounce back from overwhelm and bounce forward to emotional re-centring, an independent mindset and creative expansion. The intention was not for you to simply air your emotions but to address them with compassion, and then redirect your energy to more creative change endeavours.

Here's a quick recap of the main ideas in each chapter:

CHAPTER 1: REALISE YOUR REALITY

- Your human state of change determines your relationship with change.
- Your change leader status puts you at greater risk of burning out between six months and two years.

CHAPTER 2: RESPOND VIA YOUR CAPABILITY

- Your conscious awareness and subsequent choices shape your reality.
- Your change capability needs to level up if you aspire to *lead* the change.

CHAPTER 3: RECLAIM YOUR BRAIN

- Your experiences can be viewed through the lens of stress, over-whelm and homeostasis.
- Your growth mindset and mental strength are possible thanks to your malleable brain.

CHAPTER 4: REGENERATE YOUR BODY

- Your nervous system is overstimulated.
- Your trauma response and fears need to be attended to.

CHAPTER 5: RECODE YOUR MIND

- Your subconscious mind is the gatekeeper of your beliefs.
- Your mindset orientation will determine your success.

CHAPTER 6: REIMAGINE YOUR CREATIVITY

- Your imagination and creative mind are a limitless competitive edge.
- Your creativity can be unleashed in the flow state.

And that brings us to the here and now. You've successfully worked through the 6R model to *Reimagine Change*, but there are three more Rs I'd like you to consider. I encourage you to take the time to answer these questions thoughtfully and honestly.

- **Reflection:** *What insights most resonated with you as you were reading Reimagine Change?*
- **Refocus:** *What do you REALLY want to work towards to Reimagine Change?*
- **Re-energise:** *What decisive action are you now going to take as a result of reading Reimagine Change?*

Regardless of what you wrote down, all that matters is that you are eager to shift forward. As Mark Zuckerberg states, 'The biggest risk is not taking any risk. In a world that's changing really quickly, the only strategy that is guaranteed to fail is not taking risks.'

FOUR FINAL FOCUS AREAS

As you set off, here are four final focus areas to keep in mind.

1. SET YOUR INTENTION

Don't get caught up in quick fixes. You want to focus your attention on change that is going to be sustainable. What intention can you make today that will hold strong tomorrow, next week, next month and even next year? Remember, you are playing the long game. So, get crystal clear on your priorities. In the book, I shared that *doing less* and *being more* is the secret here. Focus in on who you are intentionally becoming and be that person. Align future you (who you want to become) with current you (the you reading this book right now). Intention builds tomorrow's value today.

2. GUARD YOUR ATTENTION

In a world of change, it is easy to get swept up in the tsunami when you are distracted by drama, defaults and duties. Rather than over-indexing on productivity tips, use a simple balancing equation linked to the human need of certainty. Ask yourself: What is my personal ratio of change and stability? In other words, don't try to change everything at once. That would put you at greater risk of spiralling or self-combusting. You need to soothe your irrational mind by reassuring it that while there is change, there is also a level of trustworthy sameness. Be your own positive enabler.

3. STRENGTHEN YOUR MOTIVATION

Don't get distracted by the next shiny new thing. *Do* keep going back to your 'why'. Keep asking: Why is my contribution to the change agenda a primary goal? It is common for individuals to leave organisations when they realise their personal values are misaligned with the organisational purpose or mission. If that happens to you, gracefully detach and deploy yourself elsewhere. Life is short – don't get stuck in the quicksand of drama, toxic bosses or falsified organisational cultures. Stand up, level up and use your voice to connect with like-minded individuals, networks and organisations that share the same values as you.

4. TRACK YOUR MOMENTUM

When you are adopting and integrating new ideas, methods and practices, you will begin to notice a shift. This may be gradual, yet noticeable, or it may be rapid and radical. The difference is in the difference. That difference is you. I believe in you, and I believe you now have the inner resources to *Reimagine Change.* All it takes is the intention to get started and set off. Whatever you do, don't do nothing. That would be a complete waste of your time, your energy and your potential. Start by making changes within yourself and then watch those changes ripple out to others.

Give yourself permission to start where you need to. Whether this is a physical break to cultivate mindful solitude, journaling your fears or self-limiting beliefs, or unearthing your creativity. My wish is that by reading *Reimagine Change,* you truly do reimagine change – in all facets of your life. May it bring you peace of mind, as well as the purpose and passion to coach yourself and others through the personal challenges and opportunities that exponential change presents.

I look forward to reconnecting soon.

Ciara x

BEYOND THE PAGES

'The darkest of nights produce the brightest stars.'
– JOHN GREEN

A dult learners have a variety of learning styles that should be appreciated and catered for. For some, the act of reading a physical book is a wonderfully nourishing experience. Others may prefer to consume content on an e-reader, or perhaps via self-paced micro-learning modules. With this in mind, I am pleased to share that the content contained in *Reimagine Change* is also available in the form of an e-book and an online program.

The art of self-leadership and change leadership often requires courage, connection and constructive feedback. You don't have to go it alone. If you and your team are interested in joining a community of like-minded individuals interested in impacting the change agenda in a more conscious, caring and creative way, then head online to reimaginechange.com.

Know that committing to and carrying out personal change capability upskilling is no easy feat. It requires full self-disclosure and perseverance. When you intentionally build your change capability, you'll change for the better – something everyone deserves.

One final word of encouragement. As human beings, it is human nature to experience mishaps, failures and falling off the wagon. When that happens, be sure to rediscover the chapters in this book, which can help you regroup and rechart a more optimal change course forward.

In the interim, remember the best place to start is to start!

Take care,
Ciara Lancaster

Reimagine Change
Reimaginechange.com
info@reimaginechange.com

SOURCES

DEDICATION
Barks, C. (May 2004) *The Essential Rumi*. Harper Collins Publishers Inc.

INTRODUCTION
Edelman, R. (2020) '2020 Edelman Trust Barometer Report', Edelman Intelligence. www.edelman.com

Schwartz, T. and Pines, E. (July 2019) 'Leading on Empty: How Leaders Drive Their People To Burnout'. www.forbes.com

Moss, J. (December 2019) 'Burnout Is About Your Workplace, Not Your People'. Harvard Business Review. www.hbr.org

Luthans, F., Youssef, C., Avolio, B. (August 2006) *Psychological Capital: Developing the Human Competitive Edge Kindle Edition*. Oxford University Press.

Clark, S. (November 2010). 'The Ashes 2010: What Merv Hughes told me about the emu and kangaroo'. https://www.theguardian.com/sport/blog/2010/nov/25/the-ashes-2010-stuart-clark

CHAPTER 1: REALISE
American Psychological Association (May, 2017), 'Change at Work Linked to Employee Stress, Distrust and Intent to Quit'. www.apa.org

Ashkenas, R. (April 2013) 'Change Management Needs to Change'. Harvard Business Review. www.hbr.org

Cavanaugh, A. (November 2019) *Contagious You: Unlock Your Power to Influence, Lead, and Create the Impact You Want*. McGraw-Hill Education.

Flora, C. (July 2019) Psychology Today article 'Protect Yourself from Emotional Contagion'. https://www.psychologytoday.com/au/articles/201906/protect-yourself-emotional-contagion

Garton, E. (April 2017) 'Employee Burnout Is a Problem with the Company, Not the Person'. Harvard Business Review. www.hbr.org

Gleeson, B. (July 2017), '1 Reason Why Most Change Management Efforts Fail'. Forbes. www.forbes.com

Kotter, J. P. (September 1996) *Leading Change*. Harvard Business School Press.

Littlefield, L. (November 2015) 'Stress & Wellbeing: How Australians are coping with life'. The findings of the Australian Psychological Society Stress and Wellbeing in Australia survey. www.psychology.org.au

Marsh, J. and Ramachandran, V.S. (March 2012) 'Do Mirror Neurons Give Us Empathy?'. Published by the Greater Good Science Centre at UC Berkeley. https://greatergood.berkeley.edu/article/item/ do_mirror_neurons_give_empathy

Puleo, G. (March 2014) 'Burnout and post-traumatic stress disorder'. TEDx Seton Hill University. TEDx Talks Youtube.com.

Senniger, T. (2000) 'The Learning Zone Model – ThemPra Social Pedagogy' http://www.thempra.org.uk/social-pedagogy/key-concepts-in-social-pedagogy/ the-learning-zone-model/

Vygotsky, L., Cole, M., John-Steiner, V., & Scribner, S. (1978) *Mind in Society*. London: Harvard University Press.

CHAPTER 2: RESPOND

Cannon-Brookes, M. (June 2017) 'How you can use impostor syndrome to your benefit'. TEDx Sydney. TEDx Talks Youtube.com.

Carter, S. (July 2014), 'Are you suffering from compassion fatigue?' Psychology Today.

Chamorro-Premuzic, (March 2019) 'Why do so many incompetent men become leaders?' TEDx University of Nevada. TEDx Talks Youtube.com.

Eurich, T. (2017) *Insight: The Power of Self-Awareness in a Self-Deluded World*. Macmillan.

Goldsmith, M. (2010) *What Got You Here Won't Get You There: How successful people become even more successful*. Profile Books.

Harrington, H. J. (2014). 'Organizational Capacity for Change: Increasing Change Capacity and Avoiding Change Overload'. *PMI White Paper*.

Jonty, P. (March 2014) *Change Fatigue: The Hidden Sleeper in Change*. Morgan McKinley.

Jung, C. G. (2003) *Psychology of the Unconscious*. Dover Publications.

Jung, C. G. (1953) *Two Essays on Analytical Psychology*. London.

Lafair, S. (January 2018) 'Here's why effective bosses are hard to fire according to Warren Buffet'. Inc.com

McGonigal, K. (December, 2011) *The Willpower Instinct: How Self-Control Works, Why It Matters, and What You Can Do to Get More of It.* Avery.

Merton, T (1988) *A vow of conversations.* New York: Farrar, Straus and Giroux

Mochari, I. (September 2015) 'Brene Brown on How to Avoid a Perfect Shame Spiral at Work'. Inc.com

Twaronite, K. (February 2019) 'The Surprising Power of Simply Asking Coworkers How They're Doing'. Harvard Business Review. www.hbr.org

MacLean, P.D. 'The triune brain, emotion and scientific bias', in Schmitt (1970) *The Neurosciences: second study program.* The Rockerfeller University Press, New York.

MacLean, P.D. (January 1990) *The Triune Brain in Evolution: Role in Paleocerebral Functions.* Springer.

CHAPTER 3: RECLAIM

David, S. (September 2017) *Emotional Agility: Get unstuck, embrace change and thrive in work and life.* Penguin Books Ltd.

David, S. (November 2016) 'Ways to better understand your emotions', Harvard Business Review. www.hbr.org

Deacon, T. 'A theory abandoned but still compelling'. Berkeley University's Yale School of Medicine. www.medicine.yale.edu.

Dweck, C. (2006) *Mindset: The New Psychology of Success.* Ballantine Books.

Fabritius, F. & Hagemann, H (2017), *The Leading Brain: Neuroscience Hacks to Work Smarter, Better, Happier.* Penguin Random House.

Gibran, K. (1963). *The forerunner: His parables and poems.* London Heinemann. (Original work published in 1920).

Kahneman, D. (July 2012) *Thinking, Fast and Slow.* Penguin Books Ltd.

Maslow, A. H. (1943) 'A theory of human motivation'. *Psychological Review.*

Maslow, A. H. (1970b) *Religions, values, and peak experiences.* New York: Penguin.

Maslow, A. H. (1987). *Motivation and personality* (3rd ed.). Delhi, India: Pearson Education.

McKeown, P. (September 2015) *The Oxygen Advantage: The simple, scientifically proven breathing technique that will revolutionise your health and fitness*. Little, Brown Book Group.

Pittman, C & Karle, E. (January 2015) *Rewire Your Anxious Brain: How to use neuroscience of fear to end anxiety, panic and worry*. New Harbinger Publications.

Rock, D. (2008) 'SCARF: A brain-based model for collaborating with and influencing others', Neuroscience Journal.

Rock, D. (December 2009) *Your Brain at Work: Strategies for overcoming distraction, regaining focus and working smarter all day long*. Harper Collins Publishers Inc.

Rodski, S. (2019) *The Neuroscience of Mindfulness*. Harper Collins Publishers.

Schwartz, J. & Gladding, R. (November 2015) *You Are Not Your Brain: The Four Step Solution for Changing Bad Habits, Ending Unhealthy Thinking and Taking Control of Your Brain*. Penguin Putnam Inc.

Seligman, M. (February 2012) *Flourish: A Visionary New Understanding of Happiness*. Simon & Schuster.

Seligman, M. (May 2011) *Learned Optimism*. Random House Australia.

The Heart Math Institute: 'The Science of Heart Math'. www.heartmath.com.

Toker, R. (April 2018) 'You don't have a lizard brain'. The Brain Scientist. www.thebrainscientist.com.

CHAPTER 4: REGENERATE

Achor, S. & Gilean, M. (2017) *Resilience*. Harvard Business Review Emotional Intelligence Series book. HBR Press.

Amy, B. (March 2020) 'The Best Way To Make Career Progress Is To Take A Break'. Forbes. www.forbes.com.

April, K., Dharani, B. & Peters, K. P. (2012) 'Impact of Locus of Control Expectancy on Level of Well-Being'. Semantic Scholar. www.semanticscholar.org

Campbell, J. (2012) *Hero With A Thousand Faces*. Princeton University Press.

Castrillion, C. (July 2019) '10 Ways to Set Healthy Boundaries at Work'. Forbes. www.forbes.com

Karayurt, Ö. & Dicle, A. (2008) 'The relationship between locus of control and mental health status among baccalaureate nursing students in Turkey'. Social behaviour and personality journal. www.sbp-journal.com

La Pera, D. (August 2019) 'Boundaries: The Ultimate Life Hack'. www.yourholis-ticpsychologist.com.

Levine, P. (1997) *Waking the Tiger: Healing Trauma*. North Atlantic Books.

Levine, P. (2020) 'Somatic Experiencing'. www.traumahealing.org.

Loehr, J. and Schwarz, T. (2001) 'The making of a corporate athlete', Harvard Business Review, vol. 79. www.hbr.org

Neff, K. (2015) *Self-compassion: The proven power of being kind to yourself*. WM Morrow.

Neff, K. (2003) 'Self-compassion: An alternative conceptualization of a healthy attitude toward oneself'. 2:2, 85-101. Taylor & Francis Online. www.tanddon-line.com

Porges, S. (2011) *The Polyvagal Theory: Neurophysiological Foundations of Emotions, Attachment, Communication, and Self-regulation*. WW Norton & Co.

Porges, S. W. (1995) 'Orienting in a defensive world: Mammalian modifications of our evolutionary heritage. A Polyvagal Theory'. Psychophysiology, 32, 301–318.

Porges, S. W. (1997) 'Emotion: An evolutionary by-product of the neural regulation of the autonomic nervous system'. In Carter, C. S., Kirkpatrick, B. & Lederhendler I. I. (Eds.), *The integrative neurobiology of affiliation*. Annals of the New York Academy of Sciences, 807, 62–77.

Porges, S. W. (1998) 'Love: An emergent property of the mammalian autonomic nervous system'. Psychoneuroendocrinology, 23, 837–861.

Porges, S. W. (2001) 'The Polyvagal Theory: Phylogenetic substrates of a social nervous system'. International Journal of Psychophysiology, 42, 123–146.

Rosenberg, M. (September, 2003) *Nonviolent Communication: A Language of Life: Life-Changing Tools for Healthy Relationships*. Puddledancer Press.

Solnit, R. (March 2017) *The Mother of All Questions*. Haymarket Books.

Van Dam, N. & Van de Helm, E. (February 2016) 'There's a Proven Link Between Effective Leadership and Getting Enough Sleep'. Harvard Business Review. www.hbr.org

Varmam, P. & Meaklim, H. (March 2019) 'Four ways sleep deprivation affects your brain and your body'. RMIT University article. www.rmit.com.

Wakeman, C. (December 2018) 'Ditch the drama: How to live happy in a messy world'. TEDx Omaha. TEDx Talks Youtube.com.

Worline, W & Dutton, E. (February 2017) *Awakening Compassion at Work: The Quiet Power That Elevates People and Organisations.* Berrett-Koehler Publishers.

CHAPTER 5: RECODE

Baer, T., Heiligtag, S. & Samandari, H. (May 2017) 'The business logic in debiasing'. www.mckinsey.com.

Diaz, C. (January 2019) 'The Marvellous Properties of Gamma Brain Waves'. www.mindvalley.com.

Dispenza, J. (2012) *Breaking The Habit of Being Yourself: How To Lose Your Mind and Create a New One.* Hay House Inc.

Hayley, J. (1993) *Uncommon Therapy: Psychiatric Techniques of Milton H. Erickson M.D.* WW Norton & Co.

Jung, C.G. (2003) *Psychology of the Unconscious.* Dover Publications Inc.

Murphy, J. (1989) *The Power of Your Subconscious Mind.* Penguin Group.

Rodriguez, K. (August 2016) 'How To Hack Your Brain For Creative Ideas Before You Even Get Out Of Bed'. Fast Company. www.fastcompany.com.

Sandberg, S. & Grant, A. (2019) *Option B: Facing adversity, building resilience, finding joy.* Ebury Publishing.

Sivers, D. (2010) 'How to start a movement'. TED Talk. www.ted.com.

Smith, D. (June 2103) *Monkey Mind: A Memoir of Anxiety.* Simon & Schuster.

Swart, T. (2019) *The Source: Open your mind, change your life.* Ebury Publishing.

Tolle, E. (2011) *The Power of Now: A Guide to Spiritual Enlightenment.* Hachette Australia.

Yapko, M. (2020) 'Hypnosis and positive psychology'. www.yapko.com.

CHAPTER 6: REIMAGINE

Cherry, K. (July, 2019) 'Gardener's Theory of Multiple Intelligences'. Very Well Mind. www.verywellmind.com.

Chopra, D. (July 2012), '5 Steps To Setting Powerful Intentions'. www.chopra.com.

Corazza, G. (March 2014) 'Creative Thinking: How to generate out of the box ideas'. TEDx Roma. TEDx Talks Youtube.com.

Csikszentmihalyi, M. (2008) *Flow: The Psychology of Optimal Experience*. Harper Collins Publishers Inc.

Dilts, R. (1995) *Strategies of Genius*. Meta Publications.

Forleo, M. (2019) *Everything Is Figureoutable*. Portfolio Penguin.

Gardner, H. (2011) 'Frames of Mind: The Theory of Multiple Intelligences'. Basic Books.

http://www.robertjsternberg.com/investment-theory-of-creativity

Kotler, S. (1995) *The Rise of Superman: Decoding the science of ultimate human performance*. Quercus Publishing Plc.

Kotler, S. (December 2016) 'How to open up the next level of human performance'. TEDx ABQ. TEDx Talks Youtube.com.

LeDoux, J. (July, 2015) *Anxious: Using the Brain to Understand and Treat Fear and Anxiety*. Viking publishing.

Levitin, D. (2015) *The Organized Mind: Thinking Straight in the Age of Information Overload*. Penguin UK.

Lukens, M. (October, 2015) 'How To Tap Into The Neuroscience of Winning'. Fast Company. www.fastcompany.com

Mackay, J. (July 2019) 'How to bounce back from creative burnout'. www.fastcompany.com.

Nussbaum, B. (2013) *Creative Intelligence: Harnessing the Power to Create, Connect and Inspire*. Harper Business.

Pate, D. (January 2020) 'The Skills Companies Need Most in 2020'. LinkedIn Learning Blog. www.learning.linkedin.com.

Peper, E., Gibney, K. H. & Holt, C. (2002) *Make Health Happen: Training Yourself to Create Wellness*. Dubuque, IA: Kendall-Hunt.

Rhimes, S. (March 2016) 'My year of saying yes to everything'. TED Talk. www.ted.com.

Ritchie, J. (November 2017) 'Five Ways to Cultivate Curiosity and Tap Into Your Creativity'. Forbes. www.forbes.com.

Robbins, M. (2017) *The 5 Second Rule: Transform Your Life, Work, and Confidence with Everyday Courage*. Savio Republic.

Robinson, K. (2009) *The Element: How finding your passion changes everything*. Penguin Putnam Inc.

Rodski, S. (2019), *The Neuroscience of Mindfulness*. Harper Collins Publishers.

Sternberg, R. J. & Lubart, T. I. (1991) 'An investment theory of creativity and its development'. Human Development, 34(1), 1–31. http://www.roberjsternberg.com/investment-theory-of-creativity

Ursrey, L. (June 2014) 'Why Design Thinking Should Be At The Core Of Your Business Strategy Development'. Forbes. www.forbes.com.

VIA Institute on Character (2020) 'Creativity Character Strength'. www.via-character.org.

Wheal, J. (December 2013) 'Hacking the GENOME of Flow'. TEDx Venice Beach. TEDx Talks Youtube.com.

CONCLUSION
Tobak, S. (October, 2011) 'Facebook's Mark Zuckerberg – Insights for Entrepreneurs'. CBS News. www.cbsnews.com.

ABOUT THE AUTHOR

CIARA LANCASTER, a former Big 4 Professional Services Change Executive, is an author, speaker and change capability coach. Ciara is the creator of the *Reimagine Change* six-step framework – a book, e-book and online program designed to help aspiring change leaders overcome overwhelm, change fatigue and burnout through intrapersonal upskilling. Her mission is simple: To recognise and rehumanise individuals to lead change by design, not default.

Reimagine Change offers fresh and unique insights into this topic, as Ciara combines her corporate background and firsthand experience with in-depth research and commentary.

Prior to her own brush with burnout, Ciara worked at Deloitte, Bauer Media, Southern Cross Austereo and News Corp. Ciara holds a Bachelor's degree in Liberal Studies (Psychology & Economics) from Sydney University, a Post Graduate Certificate in Organisational Change Management from the University of New South Wales, and a Diploma of Modern Psychology (Coaching, Emotional Intelligence, Neuro Linguistic Programming and Clinical Hypnotherapy) from The Mind Academy. She also holds a certificate in Compassion Cultivation Training from Stanford University's Center of Compassion and Altruism Research and Education (CARE), and is a member of the Change Management Institute.

On top of writing, coaching and upskilling, Ciara lives in Sydney, Australia, with her partner and two energetic boys. Find out more about Ciara Lancaster at www.reimaginechange.com.

A portion of book proceeds will be donated to suicide prevention charity R U OK?

Printed in Australia
AUHW012351050820
331810AU00011B/11